BODY LANGUAGE + FACE RAS

READ
PEOPLE
DEEPER

Rose Rosetree

How Accurate Are Rose's Readings?

In more than 800 media interviews, Rose Rosetree has put her techniques – and professional reputation – on the line. Just how accurate has she been?

"I decided to send her a picture of myself... with the caveat that my wife would 'check' her report for accuracy. 'She's got your number,' was my wife's simple response." — The Catholic Standard

"Rose Rosetree can spot a potential fibber a mile away. Or, in this case, 2,400 miles away." — Las Vegas Sun

"Your readings for the Kalamazoo Gazette were the most amazing thing I've ever seen in a newspaper. I'm in politics myself. I know these people." – Michigan politician

"Capetalk Radio," So. Africa, "You haven't been reading my face, you've been checking with my Mum." – John Maytham

"Tony and Julie," BBC radio, *"Usually I debunk anything spiritual but... you really didn't know me before seing my photo? Your reading was like listening to my mother."* – Brendan O'Connor

"XZone Radio," Syndicated, You have more credibility with me as an aura reader than any others I've interviewed." — Rob McConnell

For an interview in the Chicago Sun-Times, Rose described Steven Colbert as "more devout than most people, and he cares deeply about being good. It's not necessarily what you'd think watching him. He's not a zealot, but really wants to be a good boy."

Months later, Parade Magazine published an interview with Colbert, including this interesting fact: He is a devout Catholic who teaches Sunday School.

How Specific Are Rose's Readings?

Skeptics worry that readings supply vague generalities, applicable to anyone. Oh, really? From Rose Rosetree's files....

"Oh MY GOD!!! I don't think you could've been any more right on!!! I am stunned!! Recovering alcoholic/drug addict, self-absorbed, our for just himself, completely snowed me with charm when I met him then turned into an evil, nasty man, almost overnight. Or maybe that was what he was to start with and just had a good act going.

"He fooled everyone who met him, too. All my family, my friends thought he was the best. I have been so confused about what happened between us. This really clears up a lot of stuff."

"I am humbled and honored to have received this reading from you. I cried in a 'coming home' type of way, when someone really knows you and receives you with great compassion."

From a student who had studied face reading for years, "Your system... is much more specific and enhanced, covering so many more aspects of the face."

"You instantly put your finger on things that it has taken me years to realize! And you threw some surprises in as well."

"I just couldn't imagine at the time of ordering (a bit reluctantly... as you never know what you get on the Internet...) how accurate your readings would end up to be. It sure was worth it!"

*"One of the staff in Starbucks ran over to me and told me that they were telling another customer about my face reading. That customer wants my phone number because she **needs** a personal consultation **right away!** You must really be good, Rose. Your freshman student already has a job!"*

Acknowledgments

Can you remember the thrill of discovering body language? My introduction came courtesy of Brandeis Professor Richard Katz in 1968. Dick was one of the best teachers I have ever had. And how appropriate that this course was offered at a school whose motto is "Truth even unto its innermost parts."

A deeper kind of truth, face reading, was introduced to me later by Timothy Mar in 1975. Physiognomy became my hobby. Years later, I camped out at the Library of Congress for weeks, surveying every book I could find in the English language. By 1986, I was ready to turn pro, teaching my system of Face Reading Secrets®.

The third form of deeper perception in this book, Aura Reading Through All Your Senses®, came to me in bits and pieces. I've had many teachers but none of them specifically taught me aura reading. The ability grew without my being much aware of it until, in 1986, I taught some friends just for fun. Soon I was teaching workshops on this topic, as well as face reading and other specialties in the field of deeper perception.

Regarding my style as a teacher, I owe enormous gratitude to my former guru, Maharishi Mahesh Yogi. For the 17 years I taught Transcendental Meditation, I was being apprenticed in how to teach subtleties of personal growth both systematically and accessibly.

Many former TMers have become distinguished teachers and writers on their own, including Deepak Chopra, John Gray, Barbara DeAngelis, and the late, sweet, Peter McWilliams.

After I, too, began teaching on my own, I have found that discoveries were just pulled out of me. For this, I thank every reader, every student, who has asked a sincere question.

Yes, teachers soon learn to distinguish sincere questions from inquiries that come as idle chit-chat or interrogations from the occasional student who seeks to joust rather than learn.

Having taught personal development for 38 years now, I've managed to catch onto this. I do count myself fortunate that nearly all of my students around the world have truly wanted to learn.

Often I have found myself at the leading edge of the New Age. Sometimes I'm asked where the innovations come from. All those years of meditation didn't hurt. I learned how to contact a level of life where anyone can get answers with the highest possible truth value. One name for that level is *ritam bhara pragya*.

To help readers access the deepest truth possible, I developed a truth-finding technique related to deeper perception, "Plug-in and ask." In this book, it's presented as a way to read auras in depth and detail.

For years, I'd been using a variation of that technique to read auras and, as well, to discover practical applications of body language and face reading. Because plug-in techniques are so accurate. I decided to research the nitty-gritty questions that matter most for real-life relationships.

Incorporating these discoveries into my work with clients and students, I felt encouraged to write this book. To update my knowledge about body language, I returned to the Library of Congress. My best finds are listed in the bibliography and I especially want to acknowledge here the two best writers I've found in the field, the astute Dr. Martin Lloyd-Elliot and the highly observant Joe-Ellan Dimitrius.

But my most important discoveries always have come from the combination of personal seeking, research into consciousness, and sincere questions from students and clients.

Was this business partner going to be trustworthy? Would counseling help that marriage? How could a hurting heart be healed? Which strengths showed, despite all the problems?

Thank you, inquiring minds that really wanted to know.

I dedicate this book to the curiosity in my students' eyes.

Read People Deeper

by Rose Rosetree

Illustrations by Meike Müller

CONTENTS

Interact

Share your experiences with this book at our lively blog community. You can find **Deeper Perception Made Practical** at www.rose-rosetree.com/blog.

Also, you can supplement your experience of this book by reading articles and FAQs at Rose's website, www.rose-rosetree.com.

Games for a Higher Social IQ

Foreword

How would your life change if you had uncanny, bulls-eye accuracy about people? I've waited a long time to see a book that gives people practical, reliable tools to attain the really important insights about their love partners and work associates. Well, it's here.

If you don't know Rose Rosetree, I'm privileged to introduce you. Rose is the genuine article, a person whom you can trust to assist you in discovering the intricate, unique and loveable "you" inside.

For nearly 20 years, I've watched her help clients grow and deepen, gaining significant insights about themselves and those around them, through her teaching them the important skills you'll discover in this book.

While Rose reads the impressive qualities of your aura, interprets the underlying meanings of your face and tells you about the subtle nuances of your body language, you feel like you're being talked to by a genuine and caring person who has your deepest interests at heart. It just feels good to be around Rose Rosetree.

We've all met folks who pride themselves on how well they judge people. And sometimes that's just what it turns out to be, pure judging with a disappointing undertone of superiority. You'll find neither that judgment nor that undertone with Rose. She brings to you — in her sessions, in her workshops, and in this book — a genuine intention for you to live a happier and more love-filled life.

Her intent is contagious, helping you to open up your best talents for really knowing the important people in your life.

You'll find practical ways to read yourself and your business associate or lover — insights that you can use right now — whether you've been together for years or for months, whether you're just a twinkle in each other's unfamiliar eyes or your situation is more like that of two people who've been staring at each other like a pair of dead fish.

Discover the deeper truth that you've been longing to know. As the ancient saying goes, "The truth can set you free," really free to have a great, close, trust-filled relationship. It can start right here in the pages of this book.

No situation demands deep truth like close relationships. Our intimate bonds can make our lives wonderful or doom them to misery. I've spent many years as a practicing psychologist and, like Rose Rosetree, I've been blessed with the gift of seeing people's energies and reading their needs, habits and innermost urges at the deepest levels of their psyches.

In these years I've seen every kind of disappointment in relationships: Dream jobs turned into nightmares, men who become disillusioned when a fantasy love affair doesn't work out; women who repeat patterns where they feel ignored or belittled; couples who have lost their passion and, with it, much of their hope for happiness in life.

What can help to solve problems like these? First and foremost, you need to be willing to learn the real truth about yourself and others. Short chapters here will help you to examine 50 key topics for compatibility in relationships. If this is your first book by Rose, I'll let you in on a secret. On nearly every page you'll learn something fascinating and new.

No matter how successful your career is right now, it pays to become more perceptive. What you learn about your own strengths can be just as important as your detective work about business associates.

And regardless of work success, it can be lonely without a special friend who is really compatible. My wish is this: May this book, through Rose Rosetree's expert guidance, help you to find the right people for your life, both work and play. Together, may you share a very human kind of happiness.

— Bill Bauman, Ph.D. * St. George, Utah * January 2008

PART 1

Read People Like a Pro

Incompatibility breaks hearts every day, but yours need not be one of them. Using the techniques in this book, you can avoid problems in your present love relationship… and also learn when a potential lover or work associate shows real promise.

I'm happily married now, but have been divorced in the past. Twice. And beyond my direct experience, since 1986 I've helped clients to release emotional pain over failed personal and business relationships. So I know how much it hurts to invest time, money and hope in a relationship, only to discover that the two of you never had a future.

Whether it's six months into a love affair or seven years into a work partnership, inquiring minds want to know, "Can I trust this person?"

You wake up and smell the coffee, swoosh it around in your mouth. Such a bitter brew! Maybe drinking coffee of any kind has been a bad habit.

What helps? Learn the deeper truths about the players in your life. Too many partners look just on the surface, live just on the surface, and—whether they stay together or not—doom themselves to remaining on the surface. Your willingness to read people deeper means that you can reclaim your power to have a happy life.

If you're **dating,** deeper perception is indispensable. Internet services, speed dating and the like can bring you too many choices. Wouldn't it help if you could instantly read compatibility? Use this book to tell which love relationship has real potential.

Already **in a relationship?** Learn how to accentuate the positive. Make it a relationship where you're committed... to fulfillment.

At **work,** relationships may seem even more unpredictable than the stock market. But there's no law against insider trading — of knowledge.

Part 1 gets you started at reading people all three ways, with body language + face reading + aura reading. Learn the latest techniques used by professionals to read all three layers. Then Part 2 gives you 50 different categories to choose from. Like a detective, you'll be able to probe into any relationship without having to ask the big questions questions directly. Find out, for instance:

+ Can I trust you to be loyal?
+ How do you manage money?
+ Are you telling me the truth?

Of course, you can read straight through all 50 categories. But this book was designed to help you pick and choose what matters most to you.

That's why the full set of categories is listed on the inside of the front cover, while the diagram to help you research auras has been placed inside the back cover. In between you'll find special sections and Bonus Boxes.

Bonus Boxes

What are they doing here in your book?

Bonus Boxes and special sections answer nitty-gritty questions you're curious about, like the sequence for sexual intimacy that most human beings prefer (see Pages 241-243) or tips for reading your own body language most accurately (see Page 7).

Some Bonus Boxes will help you most at work, like the instant ways to judge character in "How Much Can You Tell from a Handshake?" (see Pages 126-30).

But why go beyond body language? Most people don't. Why bother to add the more counter-culture skills of reading faces and auras?

Like Stereo, Only Better

Deeper perception has more than one layer. Each one can give you quality information. It would be a waste, limiting yourself to only the most obvious layer. Would you would watch a movie with only one eye or listen to music with only one ear?

When there's a choice, I'd go for stereo. Wouldn't you? Well, when it comes to deep knowledge, you have a *third* eye —and a third ear — if only you're willing to use them.

Not only does this book give you leading-edge knowledge about all three layers. This is also the first book to show how to use all three approaches together.

Body Language is the study of nonverbal communication, the best known form of deeper perception. In this book, you'll learn new ways to interpret how a person stands, sits, points, turns, etc. (You'll also gain surprising insights about how *you* react to life sub-consciously.)

Face Reading, though not as well known as body language, is actually easier to read accurately. Unlike expression, it can't be faked.

To read faces, you look at certain parts of the physical face, then interpret them. Features like cheeks and ears have multiple categories that can be read just like letters of the alphabet.

For 5,000 years, face readers from the East have counseled businessmen. Today you'll find face readers at Ginza, Tokyo's ultra-modern shopping district. When you read categories in this book related to money, power, and integrity, you'll appreciate why physiognomy has stood the test of time.

Auras are the deepest layer for reading people deeper. Soon I'll define "aura" in depth, but here let's clarify what auras are *not*.

Contrary to popular myth, auras are not just colors. To read auras in depth and detail, you actually don't need to see colors at all.

My techniques emphasize information, not colors. I've helped thousands of students to access this insider information. I can help you, too. The how-to's in Part 1 will prepare you to find *practical* information, regardless of whether you have previous experience at reading auras.

What else should you know up front? Usually I'll use the term **"partner"** for the person being read.

+ In your social life, a partner could be a family member, a friend (new or old), a date, or a long-term lover.
+ At work, a partner could be an employee or boss, a colleague or a customer.

I like that term "partner" because it reminds me of the old Westerns, what actors call each other just before the big shootout.

Actually, I mainly like using the term "partner" because it includes so many possibilities. For any category you choose, you, the mighty reader, will know which type of partner you want to read.

Speaking of language, this book uses **gender shorthand** like "he/she," with all due apology to my fellow English majors. Although inelegant, this is the most economical way to include everyone.

And speaking of inclusiveness, this book can help you whatever your **sexual orientation.** Male and female qualities occur in every love relationship, whether you're straight, gay, bi, or transgender. You'll know which kind of sexiness in a partner interests you.

When I promise that this book can improve your love life, that means *your* kind of love life! And, yes, you can read for the sake of your work life instead.

Do both or either. While you're at it, you might choose to tell friends what you're doing or, perhaps, you might prefer to keep your new source of knowledge a secret.

Ultimately you are the one who decides exactly how you are going to use deeper perception. My goal is to support your own choice about what matters most.

WHICH LAYER IS BEST

Now that you know you can access all three layers of deeper perception, maybe you're wondering which one is best. That really depends on the category you're reading. Using the examples given earlier:

- Body language provides the best clues to loyalty.
- Face reading is best for revealing what a person *does* with money (not always what he/she tells you).
- Regarding honesty, auras provide the most reliable information... by far.

Excited at the prospect of reading all three layers on anyone you choose? It gets better.

With practice, you can read from photographs, including Internet photos. Using the techniques in this book, you can learn more in 10 *minutes* of research than you might find in a *month* of "You've got mail."

Reading people in depth and detail can be that easy. But is it really accurate? My students (on five continents) say so. So do the clients who hire me to do readings for them.

Sure, many newbies are skeptical. They don't stay that way. On a regular basis, I receive thank you's where a client writes how his/her life has changed because of reading people deeper.

One smart way to overcome skepticism—and simultaneously build your skill—is to practice on less crucial relationships before you read a biggie like your lover or employee. Why not start with photos of couples you know well?

Or dare to revisit pix of your ex. Find those glaring incompatibilities. It can help you to smile when you put that "was" in "wasband" or reminisce over what happened to you "in a past wife." Check out that toxic former boss from a workplace photo and laugh, long and loud. Get over it, finally!

READ BODY LANGUAGE

Body language is the easiest way to read people deeper...or is it?

Sure, body language can be obvious, like when your partner is wearing a deep scowl plus a fist.

More often, though, body language is complicated, way more complicated than the other two layers for reading people deeper.

One nose characteristic at a time, face readers! One chakra databank at a time, aura readers! Simple, as you'll soon see!

As a body language reader, however, you'll need to go more complex. Accurate readings don't involve one simple clue, like the expression on your partner's mouth. To interpret that grin accurately, you'd better check out other signals from the rest of the body. Those different nonverbal signals may contradict your first finding.

The sheer **amount** of body language can be intimidating. How many expressions can show on one little face? Only about 7,000!

Each of us has our favorite expressions, whether to make or to read. Not everyone is an expert at decoding them all. To avoid mistakes, keep looking until you've collected multiple signals from different parts of the face or body.

For example, don't make a pass at a date until you've found at least four nonverbal signs of attraction. Not one, four. That's not so many, considering there could be 25 different signs. (See Page 136.)

Contradictions can abound. For true body language skills, you will need to consider mouth + eyes, legs + arms, etc.

Jumping to conclusions will help your love life about as much as if you were to physically jump ... and land on a new date's feet.

Better to stay put, keep your wits about you and show your business or love-life partner the same kind of respect that *you* would like to receive.

And talk about tricky! Despite what you may have been told, body language has limited accuracy for certain kinds of information. People you know may pride themselves on how they can always tell a liar by looking for shifty eyes, etc. Well, that's the kind of pride that goes before a fall.

Read Your Own Body Language

How about reading your own body language? You're not just anyone, you know. Here are some tips for reading that special person you know so well.

Whenever possible, use **photos** *or videos. Mirrors aren't as good because you may subconsciously shift body language while reading yourself.*

People tend to be harder on themselves than on others. So take a deep breath and be **objective,** *as if reading a stranger.*

Fresh insights are so much more interesting than same-old habits of viewing yourself. Be **willing** *to find something new, rather than repeating the usual stories that you tell yourself.*

Frankly, reading body language is a terrible approach when you aim to protect yourself from liars. A bright three-year-old can fool a grownup, and some grownups have become expert deceivers—including the very people you need to trust.

Ironically, the surest way to be taken in by a liar is to focus on expression. Instead, read body language + faces + auras.

What if *you* are the one who is tempted to manipulate others? My advice is don't… not for work, not for play, not for sex.

Sure, it's true that you can temporarily charm others by **mirroring** body language, like tilting your head at the same angle as your partner's, crossing or uncrossing your arms in synch, etc.

What will you really gain? Maybe your job interview will go great. But based on what, manipulation? Anything you fake about a relationship will bring unhappiness in the long run.

AVOID OTHER TRAPS

Three other traps can limit your use of body language. Here's how to avoid them.

First, read impartially. Don't use nonverbal communication as an excuse to project your feelings. And set your expectations aside.

For instance, resist the temptation to go gaa-gaa over your date's welcoming eyes. They don't mean you've hit the jackpot, not unless lust is all that you want in a lover.

Besides, even if you'd settle for some genuine lust, don't hook up just because you can. Investigate categories like CHARM. (See Page 72.) It could be a matter of life and death.

Second, unlike any other body language experts, I will help you to avoid the trap of **over-emphasizing** body language when deeper layers of perception could really be more useful. In general, use body language as an excellent *starting* place to read people deeper.

Third, remember, don't **over-simplify.** You may be tempted to settle for one pat answer. But don't. Body language is complex. Fortunately, there's a simple way you can gear yourself to find just enough data, neither too little nor too much. Use the power of intention.

INTENTION

What is your motivation when you start to read body language? No need to lie on a psychiatrist's couch, begging your subconscious mind to please give you a clue. Decide already. Just choose something.

One quick thought is all you need to set an intention, e.g., "I aim to gain accurate knowledge about this person."

Once you ask inside, automatically, your **inner self** will respond. Your subconscious mind and Wise Mind, together, form that inner self. Intention works it just like a computer. Intention acts like a search function, bringing up the data you have requested.

How else can you use the power of intention to read people deeper? Remind your conscious mind to stay open. Dismiss any urge to judge quickly to get things over with. Learning the truth about people takes more time than settling for stereotypes. A small investment of extra time will be repaid with better relationships.

MICRO-EXPRESSIONS

To read body language like a pro, learn to catch **micro-expression**s. These are private moments that flash across faces in a split second.

You must train yourself to see them. Otherwise they will whiz by so fast — and be such a contrast — that you miss the show.

Why? Think about having your picture taken. Even when you pose to look your best, sometimes a camera can catch you blinking or with a distinctly unflattering expression that you never knew you could make.

This isn't the camera's fault, you know. Nor is it some weird pathology, afflicting you alone. Even professional models don't look good in every shot. During and after photo shoots, "off" moments happen to everyone. People learn to tune out them out and focus instead on *patterns* of expression, ignoring exceptions.

Here's a second reason why you may usually miss micro-expressions. Strange but true — most of the faces you examine closely don't belong to "real" people.

Omigod, who are you seeing then? Actors and models.

Do the math! How many hours a day do you watch that screen? By comparison, how many minutes do you stare intently at real-life people, giving them your undivided attention? Is it as long as even one episode of your favorite "reality" show? Probably not.

TV performers may feel like family, but they aren't. And they don't behave normally. Folks on reality shows ham it up for the camerasl. Actors have learned to blank out irrelevant micro-expressions. (It's called "playing a role" or "staying in character.")

Do you own a DVD? Then you can prove this easily. Randomly freeze-frame a movie and you'll find super-consistent emotions being projected through each actor's face and body. Random micro-expressions are about as common as the scenes with nose picking.

By contrast, real people — not actors— show micro-expressions galore when videotaped.

The Love Lab at the Gottman Institute (www.gottman.com) is America's leading research facility for predicting compatibility in relationships. Psychologist John Gottman analyzes videotapes of couples to evaluate them.

In one famous study he used micro-expressions to predict whether couples would stay together... with an accuracy rate of 97%.

Why not set up your own Love Lab at home? All you need is a camcorder. Videotape people who interact with a lot of emotion and aren't trying to perform. Play back your recording, using the pause button freely. Wow! You'll find hidden emotions galore.

For example, *contempt* shows when the dimpler muscle, the buccinator, pulls lip corners to the side. This creates a temporary cheek dimple (more like a sneer than a smile). Often this micro-expression goes with a quick eye roll.

Once you have trained yourself to catch these split-second snapshots of emotion, you can watch them on people at the mall, at Starbucks, on subways, in airports.

An especially easy way to catch micro-expressions in everyday life is to focus on a couple interacting with another person. While one member of the couple is talking, watch for micro-expressions on the *other* one.

After you're confident at using this slow-mo skill, start to research people you know personally. Anger, embarrassment, sadness and fear are just some of the hidden emotions you'll find... even if your relationship is mostly great.

FACE READING SURPRISES

Sad but true, most people who pride themselves on reading faces brilliantly really don't. Instead they do brilliant face judging.

Alas, their skills haven't developed much since grade school, when they first learned to box people into stereotypes.

Genuine face reading isn't about **stereotypes,** superficial generalizations based on race, age, weight, attractiveness or expression.

Do you want others to stop there when learning about *you?* At worst, that means prejudice. At best... stereotypes make convenient shorthand for pollsters and plot-driven novelists.

Well, deeper perception doesn't mean using the usual stereotypes, only squinting.

You don't need to try extra *hard* to read deeper. Doing *more* of the same won't cut it. You must learn to read people *differently.*

Facial biometrics is the latest name for what you'll be reading with faces. These are physical characteristics. As a face reader, your job is to see clearly, then interpret.

Even as you read this page, scientists are engineering systems for facial biometrics. They're using distinctive data for personal identification, from bank ATMs to your personal computer.

Meanwhile, reading faces doesn't require a million-dollar research budget or a Ph.D. All you need are your eyes, your mind, your heart, and your curiosity. Each biometric item you will learn to spot has meaning to a face reader.

INCLUDE THE OBVIOUS

In the 5,000-year history of **physiognomy** (that's the fancy word for face reading) certain basics are taken for granted. But every one of them may be a surprise to you.

To read a face accurately, you must see it **on the level.** You'd be surprised how seldom people do this. When you use a hand mirror, if you're like most people, you look down at yourself.

But which matters more, resting your elbow or seeing the truth? Odd angles distort face data. Whether you look in a mirror or research a photo, make that tiny bit of effort to adjust positioning so that you can see a face on the level.

Here are some other basics about reading faces for character.

Read **one item of face data** at a time. Don't just think "big ears." Loads of categories are available for each facial feature, such as high ear position vs. low, in-angled vs. out-angled, large earlobes vs. small.

Each **category** contains one or more items of face data. Look, really look, at every category that I present in this book. Then you'll start to see like a face reader.

Reading away, you'll find practical interpretations that will prove extremely accurate. However, this is true only if the person you're reading is **old enough** for face reading to be appropriate. That means at least 18 years old.

Otherwise the face hasn't had matured enough to be readable. Still, you can read body language and auras on that youngster.

And now here comes some good news for any face reader. **Don't fuss** over what you're reading. Every item you choose to read should be obvious. If that face data isn't obvious, skip it. Go on to read body language and auras.

Why? The more **extreme** any face data, the more accurate your interpretation will be. "Extreme" means very large or small; very straight, curved or angled; very high or low, etc.

Suppose, for example, you're checking out *nostril size*. (And once you know what that means, you sure will!) Some nostrils are neither large nor small. How wacky would it be, agonizing for hours over those somewhat small specimens? You're better off skipping that category entirely.

This book contains many illustrations of face data. If you'd like to carry around additional pictures to use like a birdwatcher's guide, I recommend my how-to book, *The Power of Face Reading*.

SURPRISE!

Becoming more experienced as a face reader, you'll stop seeing in that same old, same old way you learned in first grade. Here are some of the surprises that await you.

For compatibility in love relationships, it's especially important to read **facial contrasts,** where you have something very different from your partner. Opposites attract. Find out, specifically, why.

Use the FACE READING index in the back of this book in order to research any strong contrast that catches your eye.

Next, consider **asymmetry.** People who don't read faces yet sometimes call that being "crooked." I call it being "human." Experienced face readers pays attention to what, exactly, is asymmetrical.

Since asymmetry matters, you'll need to **tell left from right** when reading a face. What's the easiest way? Pretend that you're shaking hands, right to right. Once you've mentally crossed over from one side to the next, you'll find the left side just right where it should be. So remember this quick trick. To cross over mentally, left or right, draw on your experience of shaking hands and... "Go flippo."

See Your Face Accurately

Want to read your own face? Find a mirror. Practice holding it up on the level, just as you would hold a photograph. Looking down at people is never a good way to learn the truth.

Only one thing is different when you read your own face. Because mirrors reverse our faces, the right side of your face will be on the right side of the mirror, the left on your left. No need to "Go flippo."

Often I'm asked how you can read someone who has had **cosmetic surgery.** People ask, "How can you ever find the original face?"

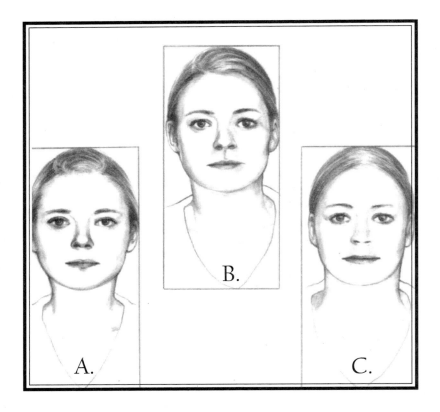

Illustration 1. ASYMMETRY

All three faces are quite symmetrical. Just for fun, let's sharpen your eye for finding subtle differences. Comparing these three faces, A., B. and C., which one has:

1. Just one close-set eye.
2. Different eyebrow heights, with her left brow higher.
3. Different nostril shapes, one round, one rectangular.
4. Cheeks wider on one side

For answers, turn the page.

Why assume that you need to? The face that person bought with the coin of the realm, what do you think that is, chopped liver?

For reading character, a person's current face counts. And it may interest you to know that some face readers believe that surgery on the outside changes the person within.

You know, faces evolve over time. It happens whether there has been surgery or not. And here's a romantic fact of life you may never have considered. If you and that partner stay together long-term, if you're really compatible, *eventually* the two of you will come to look more alike physically.

Similarly, if your work is the most important part of your life, and you greatly admire a business partner, you'll get the long-term dividend physically. Over time, your faces will come to look more alike.

The face really does reflect the soul. And, just as souls evolve over time here at Earth School, faces change in ways that are 100% meaningful.

Worried about Looking Older?

Read your face as it is now. Give yourself credit for all the specific talents that correspond to your face data.

Then find a comparison photos from your family album and look for specific facial changes. This book can help you to interpret many of them.

Read a picture of the old you, then check the mirror for what you have now.

Interpret as a face reader, not how advertisers want you to see. Immunize yourself against social pressure to "Buy, buy, buy" makeup or clothing or surgery.

Then, if reading faces for character doesn't do enough to build your confidence, start reading your aura.

WHY YOU CAN READ AURAS

Your **aura,** the electromagnetic energy field around your physical body, has layers like an onion. Only, of course, you smell better.

Auras are made of subtle energy, so you can't read them until you make the (slight) effort of shifting out of everyday perception and into something deeper.

Hopefully, this will soon become a pleasant shift for you, akin to "Let's slip into something a little more comfortable."

Reading auras, you'll benefit from the fact that they contain centers of concentrated information called **chakras.** (Pronounce the word either as CHAH-kraz, like *chocolate,* or SHAH-kraz, like *sharing.*)

I've discovered that **every main chakra contains 50 different databanks of information.** In this book, I'll teach you how to read the most practical databanks concerning business and love relationships.

Illustration 1. QUIZ ANSWERS

B.'s **close-set eye** is on her left side

B.'s **left eyebrow** is higher than her right eyebrow.

B.'s **nostril shapes** are round (right) and rectangular (left).

B.'s **wider cheek** is on her right side.

Give yourself extra praise if you happened to notice this:

+ Our middle drawing, B., was used as a basis for the other two drawings.
+ A. has her right side copied, flipped, and assembled to put **two right sides** together.
+ C. had the same process used to create a version of B.'s face made from **two left sides.**

Chakra databanks can read in many ways. In this book, I'm going to teach you my favorite way to get quality information, **plug-in techniques**.

I developed three variations, three different techniques, that make it easy for you to obtain accurate information, in person and also when reading photos.

Can you use a lamp? Then you can use a plug-in technique to read chakra databanks.

In the following pages, I'll teach you one skill after another until you're ready to plug in and read any data you like. But first, here's incentive. What kind of information can you hope to receive from an aura?

Laugh All the Way to the Databank

Each of your chakras can be compared to a bank account worth millions of dollars. But before you get too conceited about your net worth, remember that everyone else's chakras are fabulous resources, too.

Also, the wealth isn't measured in dollars or euros, but as information.

This wealth can be yours. Once you know how to plug-in and ask, you can secretly cash in on anybody's databank account... do it without depleting his/her funds... just as other people can freely make knowledge withdrawals from yours.

This free-for-all aspect is one reason why you're so smart, choosing to read auras now. Not only can you easily become as data-rich as you desire. Eventually in-depth aura reading will shift from an underground interest to the mainstream. When that happens, the partner who *doesn't* read databanks will be at a disadvantage.

I call aura reading a survival skill for the 21st century.

So go for it. Here's your chance to laugh all the way to the databank.

Illustration 2. THE MAIN CHAKRAS

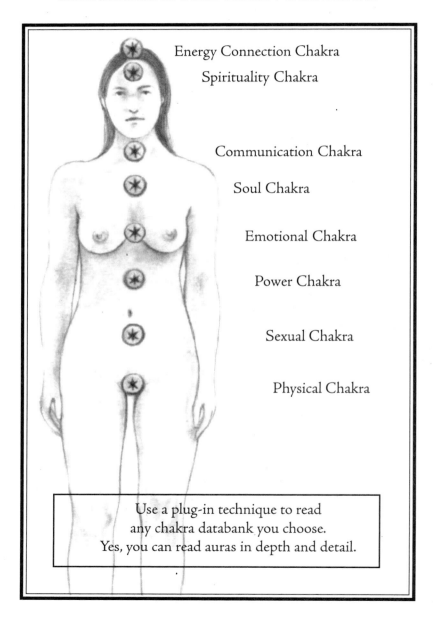

Energy Connection Chakra

Spirituality Chakra

Communication Chakra

Soul Chakra

Emotional Chakra

Power Chakra

Sexual Chakra

Physical Chakra

Use a plug-in technique to read
any chakra databank you choose.
Yes, you can read auras in depth and detail.

Whether you use my plug-in methods or you prefer to substitute some other aura reading technique, the purpose is to cash in on information. Just as you wouldn't go to a Swedish bank account for Japanese money, you need to investigate every databank in the right place. Unless you know where to find each account, you won't get a nickel's worth of knowledge.

Even people who already have tried aura reading sometimes find that they go just so far, then get stuck. Sound like you? Well, here comes the information that can help you to do the un-sticking.

Each chakra location contains 50 different databanks of information. The following list gives examples of databanks that are especially important for reading people in practical ways. (When you read the 50 different categories in Part 2, I'll always steer you towards the databanks most relevant to what you're researching, and you can find all these databanks referenced in Index 3.)

Important Chakra Databanks

1. PHYSICAL CHAKRA

Location: Front of the body, right between the legs, where the torso starts.

Sample Databanks:
+ Qualities of Sensuousness
+ How He/She Relates to His/Her Physical Body
+ Trusting Strangers
+ Trusting Life
+ Major Traumas, Have They Been Healed?

2. SEXUAL CHAKRA

Location: Two inches below the navel.

Sample Databanks:
+ Creativity
+ Expressiveness as a Communicator
+ Balance of Masculine and Feminine Energy

- Sexual Strengths
- Inner Child

3. POWER CHAKRA

Location: Ribcage area at the front of the body, beneath the chest or breasts, above the navel.
Sample Databanks:
- Integrity and Trustworthiness
- Intellectual Specialties
- Self-Confidence
- Power Strengths in Career
- Power Strengths with Love Relationships

4. EMOTIONAL CHAKRA

Location: Center of the body, between the nipples.
Sample Databanks:
- Giving Love
- Receiving Love
- Emotional Self-Acceptance
- Emotional Stability
- Stored Psychological Pain

5. COMMUNICATION CHAKRA

Location: Front of the throat.
Sample Databanks:
- Communication
- Sense of Humor
- Truthfulness
- Way of Presenting Self at Work
- Intimacy Style in Love Relationships

6. SPIRITUALITY CHAKRA

Location: Front of the forehead, above the eyebrows.

Sample Databanks:
+ Integrity in Conduct of Spiritual Life
+ Interest in Spiritual Growth
+ Quickest Path of Evolution
+ Moral Development
+ Willingness to Examine His/Her Human Life

7. ENERGY CONNECTION CHAKRA
Location: The top and back of the head.
Databanks here are not especially relevant to the 50 practical categories in this book. More useful is the following chakra.

* SOUL CHAKRA
Location: Find this little-known chakra at the upper chest, halfway between the Communication and Emotional Chakras.
Sample Databanks:
+ Degree of Fulfillment as a Human Being
+ Expression of the Soul through the Personality
+ Way of Relating to Social Obligations
+ Availability to Commit to a Love Relationship
+ Soul's Reaction to Any Life Choice You Care to Research

Permission

Sure, you have the right to read another person's aura *consciously.* You're already doing it already *subconsciously.*

Besides, your date or lover has a full set of chakra databanks, just loaded with useful information. Any prospective boss or client or business associate has a full set of databanks, too.

Before investing your time or money or hopes in any relationship, you can research "the company." Who is that person, really?

When reading aura databanks, you will find two different types of information.

Gifts of the soul may inspire you, as well they should. Each databank contains a gift, distinctive as a fingerprint and just as permanent.

Often, however, you will also find what I call **"STUFF,"** problems and distortions at the auric level. STUFF includes:

+ Short-term problems.
+ Chronic problems.
+ Dysfunctional patterns learned from childhood.
+ Structures within an aura itself that cause problems, such as cords of attachment.

Don't let STUFF discourage you. STUFF can always, always, always be healed, provided that a person is willing to do so.

Healers who specialize in removing stuff from auras include practitioners of Energy Psychology (e.g., Emotional Freedom Technique), Energy Medicine (e.g., Donna Eden's Energy Medicine Self-Care Programs), and Energy Spirituality (e.g., my 12 Steps to Cut Cords of Attachment™).

Recipes for Success

Now I'm going to teach you how to read chakra databanks. It's a small but tasty set of skills that I will teach you one skill at a time. With each set of instructions, approach it like cooking a recipe, easy as ABC:

+ Preview the how-to part by reading through it quickly.
+ Do the technique step by step.
+ Then, only then, read where I discuss the *results* from our little experiment.

Why bother to preview? Imagine that you are trying to boil an egg for the first time and you haven't read the whole recipe first.

So you pour water in the saucepan, turn on the heat. Then, oops, no egg. Out you go to the nearest chicken coop, hunting for that perfect egg.

If the hen doesn't cooperate, you could get the impression that boiling an egg involves running and screaming and pecking, altogether way more complication than necessary.

For a better experience with my recipes, get your ingredients together, know what to expect, and then follow the rather simple instructions.

If you're an impatient sort, you can turn to Page 39 and see the summary of skills I'm teaching you here, so you'll know what's coming. Or be spontaneous and play along with me. Either way, let's proceed to the first skill involved in the sequence of reading auras.

Agree to Go Within

Even for the sake of reading auras on other people, success depends upon going within *yourself.* In this way, auras are very different from body language and faces.

Inside of you, is anyone home? Absolutely! This inner version of you is technically called your **consciousness.** This part of you is awake inside, constantly having human experiences (unless you're either asleep or dead).

It's personal, knowing things inwardly, on your own. Not in a bar, with other people talking and clinking their glasses, instead you're alone, dating yourself.

How does a person know things, on your own, things about your own consciousness?

+ You have one way of knowing things *outwardly,* with your eyes open.
+ But you also have a way of knowing *inwardly,* when your eyes are closed. This version of reality is less concrete, more subtle… and also more spiritually powerful.

During my 38 years as a spiritual teacher, I've learned this surprising fact. Even blind people know the difference between *eyes open* and *eyes closed.*

Going within to use your consciousness is, therefore, the first skill of aura reading. This will be familiar to you if you have done yoga or spiritual exercises. But many otherwise sophisticated people have never learned to go within and pay attention to what they find. Now is the perfect time to begin.

Okay, I know that the very notion of going within scares some folks. Suddenly they turn into scoffers or cynics or feel an urgent need to eat an entire box of donuts.

Is your desire to learn about people stronger than your fear? Then you can do this. Dare to go within. Soon you'll emerge, stronger and clearer, also more ready to read auras.

Supplies needed: A pair of working eyelids.

You'll also need undivided attention, so turn off your cell, your TV, and background music of any kind. Also, no smoking. And no chewing gum, either. Am I strict or what?

I'm not coordinated enough to do this exercise while chewing gum. You may be, but save that for when you're more experienced as an aura reader.

Time needed: Two minutes. (Don't cheat. Use a timer, if necessary.)

What to do:

1. Sit comfortably. Have your eyes open for 10-15 seconds or so. Don't count the seconds, just give yourself a little chunk of time.

2. Then close your eyes for about the same chunk of time.

3. Continue alternating like this until the two minutes are up.

After you do the exercise, read this:

Eyes opened or closed, you noticed things, didn't you? And that's spontaneously, no trying needed. Eyes closed, you might have notice bodily sensations, emotions, thoughts, or the spiritual experience of just being. Any of this would count as inner knowing. With auras, the knowledge you receive will have the quality of inner experience more than outer.

Your Preparation Process

This technique is as easy as rolling out of bed. And as necessary, if you aim to have much variety in your social life.

You'll do this same Preparation Process every time you read auras.

Supplies needed: A comfortable chair, where you can sit without feeling like a lab rat. Ideally, your spine is pretty straight and your head is not supported. (Okay, sometimes you might choose to stand, rather than sit. Comfort is key.)

Time needed: The first time you do this exercise, give yourself 5-10 minutes. Once you're comfortable with it, you'll need more like 5-10 seconds.

What to do: Switch on your inner awareness. Aura reading depends on the knower even more than the person being read, so the clearer you are inside, the better your reading will be.

1. **Close your eyes.** Okay, you might have to open your eyes sometimes to peek at the rest of this recipe. Do this as needed but then quickly close your eyes again. Soon you'll know the whole procedure by heart.

2. Take some **vibe-raising breaths,** slow and deep: *In through the nose, out through the mouth.* Use this breathing pattern like a rheostat to "turn up the light" whenever you read auras.

3. Still taking vibe-raising breaths, use awareness to **pay attention to your body,** head to toe. Linger over the experience of what it feels like to be you. Know that effortless self-awareness, like noticing sensations in your body, is the basis of aura reading. Trust it.

4. Ah, now you can return to **normal breathing.**

5. **Get Big** by connecting with your spiritual source. If you already have a way that works for you, fine. Otherwise, just think the sentence "God, connect with me clearly now." Think this "Get Big sentence" just one time, in your head.

Automatically (in a subtle but very real way), your consciousness will expand, bringing the greatest possible accuracy to your aura reading.

6. **Set an intention.** Think something like, "Help me to learn more about this person."

In every section of Part 2, I'll supply a specific intention that relates to the research you're doing. No matter how experienced you become, always take a few seconds to Get Big and set an intention.

7. Open your eyes and do the **plug-in technique** of your choice. (Of course, if you haven't learned that yet, don't! Just keep your eyes open and consider yourself successful.)

Read this after you do the exercise:
Were you expecting some big, flashy result? I sure hope not. This Preparation Process is like putting the fuel in your car. Driving lesson comes next. Here is what I hope *did* happen for you:

+ You did all seven steps, without skipping any of them.
+ You didn't try to do anything extra fancy or alien. Leave extra techniques for another time, maybe for another book. Unless you do my techniques exactly as presented here, you won't find out what they can do for you.
+ You survived. So now you're ready to learn the next technique. Cool!

Choose an Aura to Read

Whenever you start to read an aura, you will need a particular someone to read. That could be:

You. Smart choice! You're a most convenient subject for the first few times you experiment with aura reading.

A willing volunteer. While you're learning, it's fun to do trades with a partner, but you could also ask a friend to serve as volunteer, helping you practice.

When I say "willing volunteer," I'm being polite. What I really mean is somebody who is not skeptical, hostile, negative, confrontational, doing you a "big" favor, etc. Even for a seasoned professional, it is no fun reading auras for someone whose game is to give you a hard time. Find somebody willing to play nice.

Anybody you want. After you have had some practice with reading auras, yes, you will be able to read anybody you choose, willing or otherwise. You can do this in person or by reading a photo, but I recommend using a photo. It's a way to avoid the full impact when the person you're reading is troubled or otherwise unpleasant.

A person in a photo. How else do you think you're going to be able to read the aura of your favorite movie star?

More important, photos are a great way to read people at work or read dates. Photos are also excellent for reading lovers or relatives.

First you will need to practice reading live people until you're comfortable with reading auras that way. Once comfortable, you will be ready for my plug-in technique to read auras from photos.

Master the Concept of Plug-In

Traditional aura reading techniques force a person to stare and strain and try really hard to be visual, even if this doesn't come naturally.

Welcome to the 21st century, where educational research has established that different people learn differently. Given these many styles of intelligence, I provide more than one version of plug-in technique.

Here's what they all have in common. They're easy, like sticking the electrical cord from a lamp into a wall socket.

Reading auras, always start with the Preparation Process. Then aim your hand or eye at the chakra you wish to read. Automatically, your awareness becomes "plugged in."

After you're nicely plugged in, you ask one question at a time. The question extracts a specific kind of information from a chakra databank. This is like using the switch on a lamp to turn it on. This is *not* like using rocket science to turn a rocket on.

Then all you need do is accept what you get.

Trust takes a bit of getting used to, but if you really want to snoop — ahem, read people deeper — you're motivated to go a bit beyond your normal comfort zone, correct?

Plug-In by Touch

Here is the touchy-feely version of reading auras. Ah, my favorite!

Supplies needed: Besides yourself, the researcher, you will need a person to read, and one chakra databank that you aim to research.

Each chakra has a location that corresponds to a part of the physical body. First time, I recommend choosing the Communication Talent databank at the Communication Chakra. (Later, you can use any databank you choose, and this book gives you dozens of chakra databanks to choose from.)

Time needed: Allow five minutes.

You're not sacrificing "the best years of your life."

What to do:

1. Start with your **Preparation Process.**
2. Choose **a chakra databank** to investigate. (Okay, this first time I did it for you, the Communication Talent databank.)
3. Plug in through **touch.** Sensitize your hands by rubbing them together briskly. Then place one of your hands a few inches away from your body at the chakra location. Hold the fingers together like a wad, rather than separating them.
4. Now that you're plugged in, **think a question,** such as "What talent does he/she have as a communicator?" Think the question in your mind, with the same tone of voice you would use for regular thinking. (Hey, in case you're wondering, your inner self isn't terribly far away. No need to shout!)
5. Immediately **release the question,** so that your inner self can answer, rather than your cute everyday personality. Aura

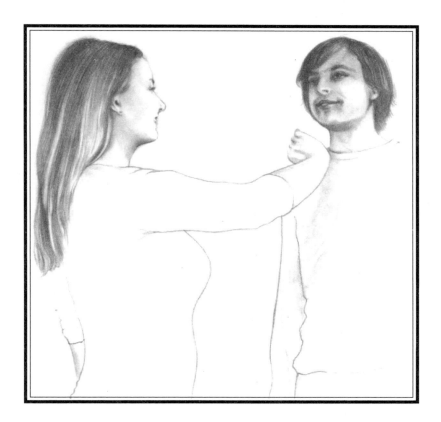

Illustration 3. PLUG-IN BY TOUCH

Meike, the illustrator, got the hand position exactly right.

+ You may choose to use either your right or left hand when doing this technique.
+ Either way, aim for a position like that shown here.
+ I notice five important things about that hand placement. Can you find them?

Answers are on the next page.

reading is, literally, a no brainer. Close your eyes. Take a few vibe-raising breaths and just sit there, being comfortably awake inside.

6. **Accept the answer.** Information will come to you. It will come through a subtle version of how you receive knowledge in other life situations.

Sure, if you're strongest at remembering people based on images or colors, that's how you'll receive your aura reading. But you may hear information or feel emotions or notice sensations in your own body or flash directly on the truth, etc. Having done the plug-in technique up to this point, whatever you get will be an answer to your question, so trust it.

7. **Give thanks** for what you received. Sometimes beginners doubt their experiences. Well, the best way to overcome doubt is gratitude. Besides, it's just plain good manners. Whomever you called on to "Get Big" is still hanging around, so say "Thank you."

Illustration 3. QUIZ ANSWERS

Here are some tips:

1. Fingers are loosely held **together**, not spread or sprawling.
2. The hand is placed **sideways**, not up-and-down (which could straddle more than one chakra location, about as useful for aura reading as straddling two lanes when driving a car.)
3. The **palm** (not the fingers) is centered at the chakra location.
4. The palm is held just **a few inches away** from the physical body.
5. The hand position is **comfortable,** not awkward. If you flip your hand around to point toward the opposite direction, that is an example of "less comfortable." Go for comfy.

Read this after you do the exercise:
Which hand is better to use for the plug-in technique? Use either right or left when you do this technique. Don't switch in the middle of doing a reading.

And never research the same databank twice to compare results, because that can be crazy-making. You have plenty of databanks to read. Satisfy any yearning for variety by reading several, some with your left hand and others with your right.

Experimenting, you'll find that one hand is easier for you to use. From now on, consider that to be "The Hand" that you use from now on for aura reading.

How do you use this technique on **somebody other than yourself?** If you're reading another person, have him/her nearby. Place your hand a few inches off the body, just as you did with yourself.

Explain in advance that you need quiet. Don't forget your Preparation Process just because somebody else is there. You'll need quiet, so avoid conversation. It could be even more distracting than chewing gum! Finish the technique before you say another word.

Regarding **position,** find a comfortable way to hold your hand at the chakra location, palm facing your research subject. Sometimes newbies hold their hands awkwardly, tense up, forget to breathe. Will this help you? Not really.

If you clench up, do the Hokey Pokey or whatever else will relax you. Then start over. The previous drawing shows a **comfortable** hand position.

Plug-In by Sight

Here comes the visual version of reading auras. Some people like this one better. Some like it worse. Nice to have a choice, isn't it? And you won't know which technique you prefer, touching or looking, until you try both.

Supplies needed: Besides yourself, you'll need a mirror for seeing yourself. Lighting is no big deal. Choose whatever is comfortable for your eyes. A wall-mounted mirror, like one in a bathroom, is just a bit easier than a hand-held mirror. If you do hold your mirror, remember to position it on the level.

For your first exploration, I recommend that you choose the Spirituality Chakra, located right at the forehead, and the databank about "Fastest Way to Evolve."

Time needed: Allow five minutes. You look good but not that good.

What to do:

1. Position yourself near the mirror, so you can see yourself at eye level. Practice looking **on the level**.
2. Then close your eyes and do your **Preparation Process.**
3. Choose a **chakra databank** to investigate. Each chakra has a location that corresponds to a part of the physical body. For your first exploration, I've recommended the Spirituality chakra, which is located right at the forehead, and the databank called "Fastest Way to Evolve."
4. Direct your eyes at the chakra location. **Plug-in!** Simply look, not trying hard to see anything in detail. It's as easy as playing peek a boo with a baby. Just make visual contact.
5. Now that you're plugged in, inwardly **ask a question,** such as "What helps me/him/her to evolve fastest?" Think the question inside with the tone of voice you'd use for regular thinking. (Hey, in case you're wondering, you don't need to move eyes over to anyone's mouth in order to ask yourself a question mentally. Isn't aura reading refined?)
6. Immediately **release the question** so that your inner self can answer, rather than your cute everyday personality. Close your eyes, take a few vibe-raising breaths and relax.
7. **Accept the answer.** Information will come to you. It will come in a natural way. Trust it.
8. **Give thanks** for what you have received.

Illustration 4. PLUG-IN BY SIGHT

The guy in this picture is plugged-in just perfectly.
 * What is he *not* doing?
Find answers on the next page.

After you do the exercise, read this:

Familiarity with inner awareness will help you to trust your aura readings; you'll do best if you meditate daily, pray, do self-hypnosis or a spiritual exercise.

Becoming familiar with your inner self won't only improve aura reading, incidentally. You'll become a more balanced person, easier to get along with. This will help you in all your relationships.

Please, don't expect some big, flashy experience. Like everything involved with auras, you're entering the realm of the subtle.

If I were coaching you in person right now, I'd prove this point by doing something that's the opposite of subtle.

Probably I'd hurl a chair onto the floor. That satisfying crashing sound is *not* what you should expect to go on between your ears. (Actually this is a good thing.)

Illustration 4. QUIZ ANSWERS

Our guy is looking right at that gal's forehead.

This is an achievement because, notice, she is aiming to make eye contact. That's women for you!

But aura reading isn't about noticing somebody's friendly expression. When doing any technique to read auras, keep things simple. Just do the technique, nothing extra.

Personally, while reading auras I'm not coordinated enough to smile at somebody, tell jokes, smoke cigarettes, chew gum, or croon a love song.

Don't consider that you're being boring when you dedicate a few minutes to doing just one thing, reading auras. You're being cool. Let Cute Guy here inspire you.

Plug-In with a Photo

These days, many of your friends and business associates post their photos online at social networking sites or elsewhere. Can you learn to read them?

Does a nacho have crunch?

After you've practiced on people who don't matter that much to you, ask your lover or client for a snapshot and read away.

Supplies needed: Read one photo at a time.

What kind of picture is ideal? It should include the person all the way down the torso. Choose a front view. Use only a photo with one person in it, at least when you're starting out.

If you're into reading every friend on every social networking site, it's possible, but you'll need one separate picture per person.

Time needed: Locating that picture may take longer than doing the reading. For that you'll need, maybe, five minutes.

What to do:

1. **Position yourself** to hold your photo up, at eye level. Your brain will process information better than if you were looking down at that photo. If you're looking at a computer screen, that position is excellent, too. Sit comfortably so you'll be looking straight at your chosen chakra databank.

2. Close your eyes and do your **Preparation Process.**

3. Choose a **chakra databank** to investigate. Each chakra has a location that corresponds to a part of the physical body. For your first time with this technique, I recommend that you choose the Soul Chakra, which is located right beneath the throat, on the upper chest. Let's research the databank about Sense of Humor. (Later, you can read any chakra databank you like, including all those mentioned in this book.)

4. **Plug-in,** either through touch or vision. Either way, remember to use the correct photo position: on the level, right in front of you.

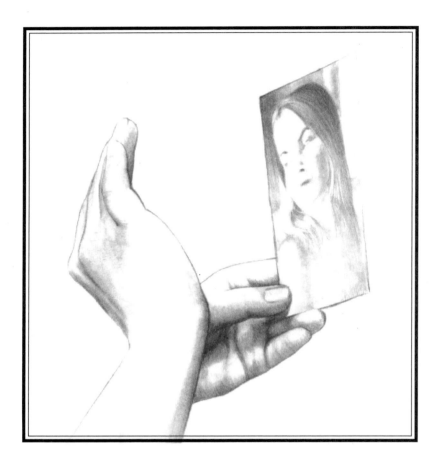

Illustration 6: PLUG-IN WITH A PHOTO

Yes, you'll definitely find it useful to read auras from photos. This illustration is supposed to show how to position your hands when you plug-in by touch.

+ What is wrong with this picture?

+ And why don't I mind at all that Meike used "artist's license" here, even if it resulted in a bit of inaccuracy?

+ What does this illustration get exactly *right* about the hand position used to read photos? (For answers, turn the page.)

+ To plug in through **touch**, sensitize your hands by rubbing them together briskly. Then place The Hand a few inches in front of that chakra location. Remember to hold the fingers together like a wad, rather than separating them.

+ To plug in **visually,** aim your eyes at that chakra position.

5. Now that you're plugged in, inwardly **ask a question,** such as "What can inspire me about his/her sense of humor?" Think the question in your mind, using the same tone of voice you would with regular thinking.

6. Immediately **release the question,** so that your inner self can answer, rather than your cute everyday personality. Aura reading is, literally, a no brainer.

Close your eyes for a moment. Take a few vibe-raising breaths and just sit there, being comfortably awake. Instead of concentrating, you're just sitting, eyes closed, being awake inside.

7. **Accept the answer.** Information will come to you. It will come in a natural way. Having done the plug-in technique up to this point, whatever you get is an answer to your question, so trust it.

8. **Give thanks** for what you received. Sometimes beginners doubt their experiences. Well, the best way to overcome doubt is gratitude. Besides, it's just plain good manners. Whomever you called on to "Get Big" is still hanging around, so say "Thank you."

Read this after you do the exercise:

Once you realize that inner experiences are... well, *inner...* aura reading becomes easy. And the more you **relax** about the whole thing, the better you'll do.

So if it helps, remember the sex counseling attributed to Queen Victoria: "Lie back and think of England."

The other way to help yourself concerns **self-doubt.** Variations on this theme include questioning your worthiness to read auras, fear of being weird or crazy, etc.

Sometimes newbies find it strange, reading auras from photos. Hey, it's no stranger than holding a telephone to talk with somebody miles away. Ever do that weird thing?

Illustration 6: QUIZ ANSWERS

Let's start with the positive. This drawing illustrates perfectly that you hold a photo with one hand and plug-in with the other.

Notice, too, that the photo is held on the level. Excellent!

Now, for the wrong parts, notice how the hand position goes up-and-down rather than sideways? Oops!

I'm quite sure the woman in the illustration was trying to position her hand at the Communication Chakra. (That's what Meike was asked to draw.) But how would such a drawing look if the hand really went sideways?

Even *thinking* about the angles needed for that kind of drawing... it's enough to make my eyes roll around in my head like little pinwheels. How about you?

The only thing harder to draw would have been trying to show the complete position for *visual* plug-in with a photo. Meike would have needed to squish into one tiny illustration both face, eyes, photo, perfect angle for holding and laser-like aim.

Thank goodness, you can use your imagination to supplement our drawing. Right? Try practicing both choices now.

- Hold a photo up at eye level. Plug-in with The Hand.
- Then put that hand down and use your eyeballs instead.

Two excellent positions for you to choose from and enjoy in three dimensions!

To overcome major doubt, take a class with someone you trust who has skill at reading auras from regular photographs.

Or you may have to resort to reading a full-length aura reading book like *Aura Reading Through All Your Senses* —ooh, how scary is that?

Summary of Aura Reading Recipes

Every six months or so, it might be useful to go back over this entire sequence. With practice, you will become completely comfortable with reading auras, on yourself or others, in person or from photos. Here is your menu of the techniques on previous pages.

- Set an Intention, Page 8
- Preparation Process, Page 25
- Choose an Aura to Read, Page 26
- Master the Concept of Plug-In, Page 27
- Plug-In by Touch, Page 28
- Plug-In by Sight, Page 31
- Plug-In with a Photo, page 35

10 Really Bad Questions

You know how teachers say, "There's no such thing as a bad question."

They're lying. Some questions are really terrible. In fact, if they were any worse, they could cause a student to self-destruct.

For reading auras, here are some really rotten questions. Even before I attempt to answer, can you figure out what makes these questions so bad?

1. Reading auras is not what I expected to see, so what's wrong?

Your expectations. It's one thing to expect your partner to have certain qualities. Research away. (That's a fine reason to read this book, actually.) But it's something else to expect that the way you *experience* auras will fit any preconceptions.

2. How come I can't just sit back and watch the colors, like watching TV?

Oh, you can, only you might be sitting and waiting for a really long time. What you have asked about is a fantasy. Now that's what some people expect for their love relationships, too. But you're not that way, are you? Let's hear it for reality, not fantasy.

3. What happened to me when I did this exercise, is it normal?

Irrelevant! What, you need to be sure you're normal before you allow yourself to breathe, or sneeze, or belch? Aura reading is just as natural as any of these, once you get over your need to do it oh-so-perfectly. Your way is perfectly fine.

4. Would other people, reading somebody's aura, find exactly the same thing as me?

Probably not. Let's not confuse hard science with the art of reading auras. For this, all that matters is your personal truth. Similarly, reading a partner, all that matters is how *you* get along with that person. Consider aura reading to be great preparation for trusting yourself in life. Period.

5. I spent 10 whole minutes on this and I haven't mastered it yet. Why can't you teach me faster?

Hey, it took some of us more than 10 minutes to have our first orgasm, too. The best things in life may be free, but some of them also require a little time.

6. Why didn't I trust myself more?

Speaking of time, torturing yourself with this question is a complete waste of time. It's like saying, when you first tried reading words, "I'm not completely confident. What's wrong with me?"

Back in the day, you could choose whether to go into psycho-analysis or just finish kindergarten. I have a hunch that you made the right choice.

Learning something really new always brings up insecurity, but don't focus on that. Banish doubt by learning.

7. How can I read auras when it is so darned noisy?

If possible, practice in a quiet room, where you have no distractions. You don't need a desert island, but neither do you need a flat-screen TV or ear buds.

8. Is it possible to be too drunk to read auras properly?

Even a little bit drunk is too drunk. Never try reading auras when you're sleepy, angry, anxious, or under the influence of recreational chemicals. In order to read auras accurately, you need to start from your normal waking state of conscious-ness.

Deeper perception is a natural kind of high.

9. Could instant messaging get in the way?

You bet. Postpone all multi-tasking until you have finished each aura reading exercise. Then you'll have way more to tell your friends.

Why is it so important to avoid any form of multi-tasking while you read auras… or faces or body language? Useful though multi-tasking can be, it guarantees that a person's awareness will stay right on the surface.

10. What if I crave absolute certainty when I read auras?

Hunt down Moses with his 10 commandments carved in granite.

Seriously, if you really need things to be obvious and concrete (a.k.a. "Taken for granite"), you're not ready to read auras yet.

That's okay. Open up this part of the book once a month and play with the exercises. When you're ready, you'll know. Before then you still can do in-depth body language and face reading, which will bring you way more insight than most people ever experience.

PART 2

50 Ways to Read Deeper

Addiction, Chemical

Avoid moving into the Heartbreak Hotel. It's way too expensive. Learn to read the signs of a drug or alcohol problem.

BODY LANGUAGE

A person must be very far gone before body language reveals addiction. Eventually he/she may **tremble,** become emaciated or beer-bellied, or reveal other obvious signs of a problem. But you'll want to learn the truth before your honey morphs into a wreck.

Likewise, at work, who wants to team up now, find out later that your partner's interesting cologne smells exactly like bourbon?

Apart from expression, eyes can give clues to being habitually under the influence. For pot, beware **dilated eyes** (enlarged pupils) when the light isn't terribly bright. For any drugs, consider yourself warned when your partner habitually wears sunglasses indoors.

Other danger signs, for liquor or drugs, are **bloodshot eyes** or eyes that are partially closed.

If you're an empath, eyes may reveal **spiritual signs** of addiction. Once your eyes meet, do you feel sickened or fearful? Deep within the eyes, that person's soul may seem to struggle, scream, or give up. Never dismiss such an experience as a weakness within yourself.

Exaggerated body language can be a sign of intoxication. Beware over-dramatic or staccato gestures, shaking, or loss of usual social inhibitions.

Voice quality may also become exaggerated when a person is under the influence. Slurred speech is only the most obvious sign. Other auditory warnings are a rowdy voice, increasing loudness, spaced-out conversation conducted in whispers, or other vocal exaggerations.

Personal **hygiene** can show the destruction of brain cells. Beware lost interest in grooming, e.g., unkempt hair, ragged nails, rumpled clothes.

When somebody has a serious drinking problem, you may also notice interesting body language around **the liquor supply.** It could be considered a new type of "business casual." A one-time employee of mine had an alcohol source that mystified me. When I saw her squirting her mouth liberally with breath freshener, one whiff told me that this would count as "minty fresh" only to others in the saloon. And it was so cute how she pretended that nothing was wrong.

Excessive patience, sad to say, constitutes another tipoff to substance abuse, especially when that patience is demanded of *you.* Ever have someone delay making a simple phone call, completing a routine chore, or sending a deliverable? And when you make a polite request after a decent interval, you're told, "Be patient."

Repeated demands that you be patient may parallel repeated rounds at the bar. And **ultra-cool body language** can telegraph, "You and your silly non-stoned reality, when will you learn to be patient?"

FACE READING

Surprise! Although faces will inform you about many things, don't rely on facial characteristics to reveal chemical addiction. Only in **myth** are the signs of alcoholism obvious. We're told to beware deep circles under the eyes, a bulbous nose or broken capillaries. Stereo-types like these are wrong, wrong, wrong. Why?

Deep circles under eyes just mean introspection. When things go wrong, someone who turns within to find a solution (or to blame himself/herself) will develop deep circles. Therefore, if you find bags under the eyes of an alcoholic, it will be an *introspective* alcoholic.

Chunky nose tips relate to valuing financial security. Keeping up a costly drug habit could, over a period of years, cause someone to develop a somewhat larger nose tip. But do you want to stick around to watch it grow?

Burst capillaries point to stress. Interpret them according to location. Ruddiness is positioned to symbolize the life area where stress is felt, e.g., burst capillaries on cheeks relate to power, burst capillaries on a nose tip are about financial worries.

Don't blame addictions, though. Burst capillaries can come from stress on the job… or be a side effect of mountain climbing.

Where *should* a face reader seek out the signs of chemical addiction? Watch **eye glitter** — how light shines out from the eyes. A dull or weird gaze can signal a problem with drugs or drink. Love that healthy twinkle when you find it!

AURAS

At the level of auras, addictions stick out like a sore thumb… to such a degree that you may suspect substance abuse even before you develop much skill at reading auras consciously.

Just one catch! If you partake of the same substance as your partner, your gut feeling may be attraction rather than alarm. A social drinker, for instance, can have a blind spot for alcoholics.

How can you protect yourself from the heartbreak of falling in love with an addict? Avoid chemical interferences yourself. Set a personal limit of two drinks per evening. Then, while you're socializing with your date, read his/her aura. (Use the chakra diagram at the back of the book for quick reference.)

Substance abuse shows in auras. In fact, chakra databanks will even unmask a **secret alcoholic,** someone who seems to put the drinks away with no ill effect.

Long-term dependence on chemicals is especially evident in the Health databank at the Physical Chakra. To investigate either short- or long-term use, begin with your usual Preparation Process: Pay attention to your inner awareness, then Get Big and set an intention to learn the truth about this person. (For more details, see Page 25.)

Plug in and ask: "How clear is his/her body-mind-spirit system?"

For a social drinker or someone who *occasionally* recreates with chemicals, aura distortion is slight. But when someone indulges often, auric deterioration becomes obvious. (Fortunately, when someone stays in recovery, that will show too.)

Another useful place to learn about chemical addiction is the Experiencing Reality databank at the Spirituality Chakra. Plug-in and ask the same question you asked before at a different chakra, "How clear is his/her mind-body-spirit system?"

With practice, you can learn to distinguish the distortions produced by different chemicals, from the uncanny, unsettling high of heroin to the dull stupor of a booze hangover. However, I'd recommend that you not go there, especially if you're an empath.

What's that? **Empaths** have a lifelong gift for directly experiencing what it is like to be other people. Until you become skilled as an empath, you're better off not doing extensive aura reading on anyone who is highly disturbed.

Whenever someone gets a temporary "high" from chemicals, the Spirituality Chakra grows disproportionately big.

It's a cheat. Coming down, the third eye will shrink faster than a certain part of male anatomy after a cold bath. For an inspiringly big spiritual consciousness, people must *earn* a huge third eye that goes with the rest of the aura.

How is that done? Do your best to make each day count. Keep yourself physically healthy and also do regular spiritual exercise.

More Fun with Drunks... on TV

Once you get used to reading how auras change when someone is drunk, you can enjoy a very sophisticated form of entertainment. It's called AURA-watching TV and movies.

Reading people deeper, you'll find it hilarious when actors play scenes where they're supposed to be under the influence.

Most viewers watch on the surface, so they'll be convinced by a few tricks of body language. But you're becoming way more sophisticated.

The actor's aura is cold sober beneath a bunch of body language tricks on the surface. It's absolutely hilarious. And you thought that watching the show was fun before!

2. Addiction, Sexual

Here's one of the bad things that can happen to good people: An otherwise balanced person stumbles into a sexual addiction. He/she falls, and falls hard, despite never having had this kind of problem before.

What is your best insurance against having this person be you? Don't confuse sexed-up infatuation with love.

With **sexual addiction,** even though most of the relationship is horrible, the physical part is great. You may find it nearly impossible to break away.

Still, you most certainly can. Hurry up and read your lover for sexual addiction now!

Regarding business relationships, is another person's sex life any of your business? Addictive sex might be. This "hobby" is unlikely to be discussed in a job interview.

BODY LANGUAGE

A variety of physical postures can show you when someone is very, very interested in sex. Yes, these are postures with all clothes still on! (See Page 246.)

FACE READING

Watch out for a **beauty mark** or **mole** located on the philtrum—that's the area between the nose and the mouth.

This mark points to an uncommonly strong craving to be considered super-sexy.

Will that take the form of sexual addiction, an eating disorder or simply dressing like a hottie? Pay attention to behavior and you can find out.

AURAS

This deepest level is best for any detective work about a partner's sex life, including research about possible addiction.

Begin with your usual Preparation Process: Pay attention to your inner awareness, then Get Big and set an intention to learn more about this person. (For more details, see Page 25.)

Plug-in at the Trust databank in the Physical Chakra. Ask, "How does he/she relate to trusting people?" Note the amount of energy available and any other information you spontaneously receive.

Next, plug-in at the Intimacy databank in the Emotional Chakra. Ask, "How does this person relate to giving love in a close relationship?" Note the amount of energy available, plus its quality.

Now plug-in at the Libido databank in the Sexual Chakra. Ask, "What is this person's quality of sexual energy?" What do you notice this time? If you find way more energy for sex than for intimacy or basic trust, uh-oh. (Unless you're reading a teenager — for them, a disproportionate interest in sex is normal, even healthy).

Pornography addictions, via the Internet, are so common today that they nearly seem normal. If you suspect a problem, don't just suspect. Read that aura!

What about your own love life? Sometimes *your* love relationship might be tilting toward sexual addiction. Research the truth in yourself, not just your lover.

How can you tell the difference between healthy attraction and addiction? The latter combines the presence of intense sex with the absence of intimacy. By contrast, a healthy sex life will bring connection at every chakra.

While sexual addiction may be fun to watch in a James Bond movie, avoid the real-life version. It's a problem, not proof of sophistication. When healthy attraction shows in an aura, it's a delight to read. You deserve no less in a lover. You deserve no less for yourself.

Could You Be Addicted to Love?

What distinguishes healthy lustiness from a sickening form of desire that could destroy your life? Research your own aura to tell the difference. Here's how.

Do your Preparation Process: Pay attention to your inner awareness, then Get Big and set an intention to gain clarity about this person. (For more details, see Page 25.)

For 3-4 minutes, talk out loud about your relationship with your lover. This conversation is just for the purpose of reading your aura. Talking on this topic will cause your aura to morph so that every chakra databank will reveal who you become while you're with this partner.

● Plug-in at the Libido databank at the Sexual Chakra and ask: "How **much** *sexual energy is flowing?" Make note of the information you receive.*

● Still plugged-in, ask: "What is the **quality** *of this energy?" Continue to record all the information you receive.*

● Now plug-in at the Emotional Receiving databank at your Emotional Chakra and ask, "How active is the databank about receiving love?"

● Plug-in at the Intimacy databank in your Communication Chakra, ask "What is happening now with my sharing intimacy in love relationships?" Record this answer.

Look over what you have found. Addiction would be signaled by a great imbalance between sexual energy and what you found at the other databanks.

I have done sessions for clients where *emotional* connection was nil (or miserably frustrated) while the sexual connection was 20 times stronger. And, of course, a relationship with sexual contact but little *communication* isn't healthy, either.

If you don't like what you find, start making changes today.

3. Anger

Would you knowingly bring home a ticking time bomb? The human equivalent is no safer, so check out hidden anger in a partner.

BODY LANGUAGE

Prospecting for anger, your first step is to stop focusing on your partner's adorable eyes. Head south. **Tight jaws** mean rage.

To learn more, focus on his/her mouth. **Muscles in lips** are part of a subtle feedback process that reveals hidden emotion.

Instinctively you may be able to read the messages of anger. It shows where lips curl, sneer or clench.

Are you new to reading the subtle signs of anger in a mouth? Educate yourself in front of a mirror. Mimic other people's mouth mannerisms. Make one face at a time, then close your eyes, take a deep breath and check out what you're feeling.

FACE READING

Anger Flags are an easy-to-read sign of stored-up rage. These vertical lines start at one of the eyebrows, then go straight up. (Turn the page for an illustration.) Don't confuse Anger Flags with the Mark of Devotion which is found at the center of the forehead, a vertical line about having a strong spiritual vocation.

On the *left* brow, an Anger Flag signals stored-up fury about a personal relationship, while an Anger Flag on the *right* brow relates to rage in the workplace.

If either wrinkle angles toward the center of the forehead, the fury has been sublimated to some degree. Still, note the pattern. (And, if it's on your own face, do what you can to release the stuck emotion. You'll feel better. Sometimes the wrinkle will fade, too.)

Illustration 6. ANGER FLAG

Notice, this counts as an Anger Flag because it starts at this man's eyebrow, rather than the center of his forehead.

In our illustration, the line moves upward from which side of his face? It's his left. (By now you're used to "Go flippo," correct?)

Because of its position, you can be reasonably sure that this Anger Flag started as a reaction to long-term problems with his wife, child, mother-in-law, or someone else in his personal life.

Question the Vanity Culture

These days, cosmetic surgeons advertise like crazy. Hey, they're entitled to sell their services, but don't believe them when they call Anger Flags "worry lines."

Folks, it's a marketing ploy. To flatter potential customers, surgeons aren't going to say, "You're chronically pissed off. I'll help you hide it."

Instead, they'll say, "Let us soothe your worry lines away."

However you interpret forehead lines (and they come in many varieties), botoxing them away will make a person numb inside. Does that sound attractive to you?

Here's another example of today's wacky vanity culture. Take another look at Mr. Anger Flag in the illustration opposite this page. He has **lowbrows**, eyebrows positioned close to the eyes. See that?

Have you ever heard that eyebrows close to the eyes signify anger? Wrong. That only happens with a temporary expression. Afterwards, the brows bounce back up, as if they were permanent press.

Look at our guy again. Is he scowling? I don't think so. His eyes haven't narrowed. The lips are relaxed. Also, the only major line on his forehead is that one isolated Anger Flag.

No this fellow isn't angry right now. He's just a man with a certain type of stored-up anger (already noted). In this drawing, he isn't showing us angry body language. He's showing us face data about long-term eyebrow position.

So what do lowbrows mean, interpreted as face data rather than expression? They indicate a talent for spontaneous communication.

This guy might be great on the radio. (Many of the broadcasters who have interviewed me live, on air, also have lowbrows. The accompanying talent is helpful for any occupation where you need to think on the spot and express yourself fast.)

Cosmetic surgeons are all too eager to sell their customers brow lifts. How much better to simply lift your consciousness! Learn to distinguish a passing mood, a significant talent, and a vanity surgeon's sales pitch.

AURAS

Here's one good thing to say about anger: Nothing in auras is easier to read. With practice, you'll quickly distinguish a temporary flare-up from chronic rage. And nobody will be able to hide anger from you, either.

Why does that matter? Concealed anger can be dangerous, crazy, sadistic or merely sad. Let aura reading protect you. Although anger can lodge in any part of an aura, the most important places to research it relate to sex, emotions and communication. It's wise to read all three databanks, even for a business relationship.

Begin with your usual Preparation Process: Pay attention to your inner awareness, then Get Big and set an intention to learn the truth about this person. (For more details, see Page 25.)

Plug-in at the Energy Flow databank at the Sexual Chakra and ask, "How does this person handle anger?"

Then plug-in at the Spontaneity databank at the Emotional Chakra and ask, "How does this person handle anger?"

Finally, plug-in at the Fight-or-Flight databank at the Communication Chakra and ask, "How does this person handle anger?"

What you find may surprise you. That includes what you find if you read those same databanks on yourself.

Anger Everywhere?

What if **every** aura you read shows lots of anger? Chances are, you're either projecting it or attracting it. Consider this your invitation to invest in some counseling. You'll be repaid with more serenity and, over time, more success at work and personal relationships.

4. Balanced Give and Take

One of the sweetest parts of love is giving... until you realize that you have been doing way more than your share. By then, a relationship may be unsalvageable. But should you catch the problem early, it's relatively easy to fix.

Start today. On the surface, everything may seem fine, but resolve to read deeper. Examine one relationship at a time. Which of you gives more? By how much? If you're the bigger giver, set new limits. If you're the bigger taker, resolve to give more.

BODY LANGUAGE

A taker may *pretend* to give, or give in. To protect yourself, start by educating yourself about smiles. A dutiful curve of the lips isn't the same as a **Duchenne smile.**

This genuine kind of smile, named after a 19th century French biologist, uses more than lip muscles. First the mouth opens wide. Then the corners turn up, pulling on *zygomaticus* muscles. These run from corners of the mouth, across cheeks, all the way up to the eyes. So cheeks will lift and eyes crinkle.

By contrast, a **fake smile** uses *risorious* muscles, which pull lips sideways, not upward. A smile like this is more likely to be crooked, too. Don't trust it.

Fabulous Fakes

Why do so many people today prefer phony smiles? Pop culture tells us they're good. Actually, they're supposed to be glamorous.

TV, movies, magazine ads, and photos on the Internet: You'll find fake smiles everywhere. Why wouldn't you? It's a fake world. Enter for entertainment, sure. But enter at your own risk.

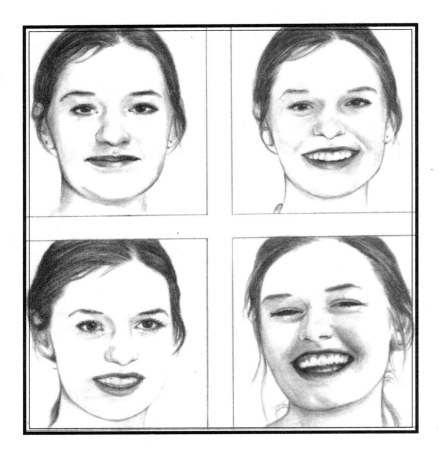

Illustration 7. Smile Depth

Physically, what makes these smiles different?

+ And what do those different smiles mean?
+ Don't count the changes to hairstyle, adorable though they are. That's Meike doing her thing, as the creative artist she is. But hairstyle readings would have to be in another book.

Answers to this face reading quiz can be found when you turn the next page.

Next time you see pix made from pixels, not flesh, remember: *"This world is not real."* In that fantasy realm, most of the smiles are phony. Hey, advertisers and photographer call the shots. Of course, fake smiles outnumber the real ones.

So here's a good follow-up question to ask whenever you see such a smile: *"What is this person trying to sell me?"*

Of course, if you're a consumer in real life, you might wish to ask the same question.

Tell True Smiles from Fakes

What I've shared with you so far about phony smiles is great preparation for the following exercise. On the feeling level, how can you tell true smiles from fake? Try this body language experiment.

1. Close your eyes. Notice how you feel inside, emotionally.

2. Open your eyes and pretend that you're saying hello to someone you love. Give a great big smile, a real one, where your lips part and you're concentrating on the other person, not the way that you look.

3. Close your eyes. Notice how you feel inside, emotionally.

4. Open your eyes and do one of those fake smiles.

5. Close your eyes. Notice how you feel inside, emotionally. Deeper perception can always help you to distinguish true from fake.

Sometimes people will give a fake smile because they're ashamed of their teeth. Hey, I understand shame. I'm a 60-year-old woman living in America in one of the most wacky. youth-obsessed cultures ever found on earth. Moreover, I work as an emotional healer.

But don't let a little dental embarrassment cause you to further cripple yourself socially. Here's my advice. Either let the shame go or take it all the way. Refuse to talk, too. Otherwise, from the moment you say your first words, other people will see your teeth.

Reading this bit of body language, real smile or fake, how can you use the information? For work relationships, don't complain about fake anything, from smiles to toupees. Just beware.

But for any personal friendship, reassure that reluctant smiler. "It's safe to open up, you know. Let your self-confidence show and grow." (Rhyming speech is, of course, optional.)

FACE READING

Smile depth can teach you a lot about habits with give-and-take. As a face reader, you explore smile depth by noticing the structure of a smile. How much does the smiler reveal physically?

Illustration 7. QUIZ ANSWERS

Once you start noticing different smile structures beyond "real vs. fake," you're doing face reading, not simply reading body language. To a physiognomist, each smile style means something.

GLAMOUR	SAVVY
Based on the smile alone, this person cares greatly about looking good and tends to be a taker rather than a giver.	This smile indicates clear boundaries about giving and receiving. The smiler prefers giving only so far, but no more.
ZESTY	**ULTRA-GENEROUS**
Showing both rows of teeth reveals uncommon zest for life, as if jumping into the pool of life with both feet first.	Smiling so big that the gums show corresponds to an inclination to give. If that's you, don't train partners to become takers.

At one extreme, a **glamour smile,** with lips closed, indicates a taker. Yes, "glamour" is my polite term for what, on a previous page, I called "fake."

Certainly, this choice of smile means that you care a lot about your self-image. Many of society's goodies go to people who have glamour smiles, and I'm not here to say that these smiles have no benefit. Just be sure to supplement what you have read here with the sections of this book about CHARM and FACADES.

At the other extreme of smile styles, consider the **ultra-gener-ous smile.** It stretches so huge that the gums show. It's the sign of being generous to a fault. In general, the more open a smile, the deeper the habit of generosity.

A **zesty smile** could be called "downwardly mobile." Besides open-ing upward, this smile style requires that you drop the lower lip down, revealing that second row of teeth. If you can comfortably smile in this way, you have uncommon zest for life.

Your potential challenge involves finding peers. How many people have told you, "You're too much"? Not your problem! For every silly-head who feels threatened by you, 10 smartie-faces will love you.

Finally we come to the **savvy smile,** where lips open fully, beauti-fully framing the upper teeth.

If you smile this way, by this point in your life you have devel-oped clear boundaries about giving and receiving. As a matter of habit, you give only so far, but no more. Excellent!

What's your only potential challenge? It's that little thing I call "a lack of tolerance for the rest of humanity."

Compared to you, all other smile styles may seem inferior. You might be tempted to smirk, but don't. For one thing, it's physically impossible to smirk while maintaining a savvy smile. Just try it. To smirk, you would have to revert to a glamour smile.

Finally, let's acknowledge the very special smile style of **a lover's smile.** This is a special kind of smile that a lover reserves just for you. The smile depth may be radically different from what is shown to the rest of the world. So when the two of you are alone together, don't just concentrate on kissing. Check out that smile depth. And then, of course, if you know what's good for you, don't stop reading there. Go on to auras.

Play Games with Body Language

How good are you at deciphering body language? Whatever your level of skill, you'll improve it by playing FACE OFF, my parlor game about body language.

FACE OFF plays up the Social IQ of yourself plus any friends you rope into participating. Actually, it may be easy to lasso them in, once you tell them how **funny** *FACE OFF is. The game can make your buddies seem slightly stewed, even when cold sober.*

Or use this as a team building exercise at work.

If you have more than two participants, form a circle. Otherwise sit opposite your partner.

Participants will take turns being IT.

Optional: Give each player a hand mirror.

1. *The person playing IT silently thinks of an emotion, the more specific the better (e.g., Not just "happy" but arrogantly happy. Not just "jealous" but hopelessly and desperately jealous). Then IT must rearrange his/her face and body to express that emotion.*

2. *All other players must mimic the expression: Duplicate everything about face, hands, arms and the rest of the body. Then turn the intensity up, up, up. Intensify and exaggerate. Push it!*

3. *Admire each player's performance. If mirrors are available, each player can peek at his/her own expression: So that's what you look like when you're.... whatever emotion that is supposed to be.*

> 4. Players take turns at naming the emotion. When all have
> finished, IT tells the players the label that he/she originally
> had in mind.
>
> Scientists have demonstrated that expression really can change
> your mood. By pasting a big smile on your face, you can tempo-
> rarily make yourself happier, while frowning will result in
> feeling sadder.
>
> Moods like these can have practical consequences. For
> instance, research has shown that after you have nodded "Yes,"
> you're more likely to buy a product shown on a TV commercial
> than if you have been nodding "No." Thus, emotions and
> expression have a reciprocal relationship. Move one and you'll
> move the other.
>
> With FACE OFF, dare I say it? You can learn even more than
> the scientists, and — better yet — do it by playing. To delve
> into deep human truths, you don't need a psychiatrist's license.
> All it takes is the patience, will, and courage to read people
> deeper.

AURAS

Here is your most accurate way to learn about give-and-take in any relationship. Research both yourself and your lover or business associate. If there are hidden problems, you'll find them at this deepest level.

Begin with your usual Preparation Process: Pay attention to your inner awareness, then Get Big and set an intention to gain perspective on giving and receiving for this person. (For more details, see Page 25.)

Reading your partner, plug-in at the Generosity databank at the Emotional Chakra and ask, "What's the pattern with giving?" Note what you get.

Staying plugged-in, access Emotional Needs, a second databank at the Emotional Chakra. Ask, "What's the pattern with receiving?" Again, make note of what you receive.

Repeat this research, only this time explore your *own* aura.

Most people have an imbalance with giving and receiving. Guess which one.

Fortunately, two big *givers* can help each other to become more balanced. One's imbalance can cancel out the other's.

Two *takers* won't stay together for long. Ever try to match two negative sides of a magnet? Expect that much mutual attraction, long term.

The trickiest combo happens when a big taker pairs up with a big giver. They can fit together like a lock and key—probably following the same mismatched pattern each one learned from parents.

If that's the case for you, don't treat this pattern like some treasured family heirloom. It ain't Wedgewood china! You have every right to smash it up, then buy into something new.

5. Charisma

A lover who makes you deliciously warm is one thing. Then there's the flame who enters your life like a human hot flash. That's sexual charisma. You could just congratulate yourself on having really good luck, except that extreme sexual *anything* can make or break a relationship.

Besides, what about the charisma factor in your work relationships?

You might be more vulnerable than you think.

Suppose a certain sexy someone slithers into your workplace. Your conscious mind says "This is work. I'm not available sexually."

But what if you still find yourself powerfully drawn to that person?

Your conscious mind may dutifully repeat, "I'm not available." Yet your subconcious self can be attracted anyway. If so, you may soon be entertaining thoughts like, "This (inappropriate) relationship is meant to be. We're soul mates."

Whoa! If you're wise, you will read that business partner deeper. And you will choose to do this *before* you start to fall in love or in lust.

In this chapter, I will refer to the person being read for charisma as "your lover" rather than "your partner." The choice of language is intentional. It's a way to remind you about the practical side of attraction. Don't let your career be sabotaged by somebody's spare charisma.

BODY LANGUAGE

For the easiest way to read sexual charisma between yourself and anyone else, pull out your camera or cellphone and take a photo with both of you together. Full-length shots work best.

With that image before you, visualize a **magnetic pole** between the two of you. This imaginary pole reveals sexual attraction. Who leans towards that pole, and how far? Does one of you lean away?

Typically the lover with less sexual charisma will lean toward the one who has more.

What if a couple is sexually balanced? When you two stand together, both will lean equally toward that magnetic pole. Even if one of you turns to look at the camera, the rest of the body will compensate.

What does it mean when one lover doesn't lean toward the magnetic pole? It can signal an attraction imbalance. This can creep up on a relationship.

Take a closer look. Yes, it's fair to keep score. Count each time that a body part leans away from that magnetic pole. Does one of you have at three more pointing parts turned toward the other. Then you could be losing power in the relationship. Count 'em:

+ Eyes
+ Mouth
+ Chin
+ Shoulders
+ Hands
+ Elbows
+ Hips
+ Knees
+ Feet

The one who plays harder-to-get scores higher in sexual charisma.

Charisma as History

The **history** of sexual charisma in your love relationship — sure you can read that. Just compare your photo now to one from the past.

Back then, did both of you move equally toward your magnetic pole? And now?

Reading Sexual Anything

Any category about sex is highly charged. Now that you've had some experience at reading people deeper, you're ready to learn why it's so important to balance what you read about sex at different levels.

Body language *is unsurpassed for showing social actions done consciously, like displaying that a mate "belongs to me."*

But you can be tricked if you only read body language, especially if read just one or two items. Probe deeper, as you've been doing by keeping score of many factors related to the magnetic pole. Remember, too, that it pays to study micro-expressions. Body language at depth can reveal subconscious factors at play in a particular relationship.

Turn to **face reading** *for knowledge about who each person really is, beyond the social roles when the two of you are together. People can play games without meaning to, and face reading will alert you when body language won't.*

Also, what you learn at this level can be especially helpful for predicting your future together. I have found that long-term, soul-level characteristics, as read from a face, are far more revealing than how a person feels about you right now.

Aura reading, *however, is by far the most important level for reading people sexually. You can learn in detail about gifts of the soul, lifelong strengths. You can also read about short- and long-term problems held aurically, what I call "STUFF."*

STUFF can always, always, always be healed. But when it's present, and your partner has no desire to heal it, STUFF can drastically distort his/her strengths as a lover. Sexual STUFF, if extreme enough, can even put you at risk to become a victim.

Can these three levels contradict each other? You bet. When they do, and you're reading anything sexual, trust most what you learn from auras.

Whichever lover is more strongly endowed with sexual charisma may pull away. Attention is withdrawn from the mate and goes out to others, as reflected in positioning of the body and face.

A flirting (or cheating) partner will turn many body parts away from the magnetic pole.

If your lover stops paying attention to you, it's hard to *demand* attention. Avoid turning clingy, either physically or psychologically. Instead, develop your own resources, with friendships and activities that build your confidence. Results will strengthen your body language, not to mention other aspects of your life.

When your strength has revived, then start planning activities that involve both of you.

Interestingly, the mark of a really secure couple is that even when they reach out to others, many parts of their bodies will lean towards the magnetic pole. Irresistible attraction really does show.

FACE READING

Gauging your lover's sexual charisma is as easy as reading **philtrum definition.** Look for two vertical fleshy ridges between your nose bottom and upper lip. This more-or-less sculpted area is your philtrum, a.k.a., overlip.

For philtrum reading, don't smile. An authentic smile may flatten out your philtrum temporarily.

Now, how much shapeliness do you find on the overlip? (For an illustration of philtrums, turn to Page 237.)

- ✦ If the shape shows clearly, you have **strong** philtrum definition.
- ✦ If the shape is somewhat visible, you have **moderate** philtrum definition.
- ✦ And if you don't see any ridges at all, your smooth overlip counts as an **undefined** philtrum.

Aha! Now you're officially a philtrum gazer.

So, how will you interpret your findings? Degree of philtrum definition corresponds to innate sexual charisma.

Should your philtrum be undefined, don't worry. Sexual charisma is only about the drool factor. Your actual mileage may vary! Besides, aura characteristics can alter your innate endowment of sex appeal, as you'll read later in this chapter.

But staying at the level of face reading, what if you lack huge, obvious sexual charisma? A potential lover will relate to you first as a friend. Thus you can establish intimacy in a relationship, then have the closeness turn sexual.

Charisma isn't about closeness. It's about making heads swivel when you enter a room. Charisma guarantees *nothing* about real-life sexiness.

What is it really like to be sexually involved with the philtrum owner, one on one? That is **real-life sexiness,** something our wacky society often confuses with sex appeal.

Blame TV, if you must find a culprit. Being a visual medium, TV portrays sexiness as owning a buff body, preferably surgically enhanced. Then characters respond according to the script. Soon any avid TV watcher gets the message. Look as much like a star as possible if you really want to be sexy.

For real-life sexiness, the body you co-create with God is perfectly acceptable. Even sexual charisma is independent of the myths portrayed on television. For instance, sex appeal doesn't really require anorexia. Have you noticed?

Still, charisma does affect a real person's love life. It doesn't have to be a matter of winners and losers. Everyone can be a winner. Reading people deeper, in fact, can help you to become a winner.

Charisma Imbalances

What happens if you and your lover have a charisma imbalance? Initially you two can be the classic case of opposites who attract. The one with the *un-defined philtrum* will feel flattered to be in the relationship. His/her sexual energy may be heightened dramatically. As for the one with more sex appeal, he/she will feel greatly appreciated.

Fast forward six months, however, and the novelty wears off. Both of you have begun to learn who each of you really *is*, in contrast to the fantasies that are common at the start of a new romance.

+ Then Mr./Ms. *Defined* Philtrum continues to attract sexual attention from his/her lover. And also receives it in public.
+ Meanwhile, Mr./Ms. *Un-Defined* Philtrum isn't receiving that public attention, and may even have reverted to old habits of not projecting a great deal of sexual verve.

Consequences of a mismatch for *Defined* and *Un-Defined* are boredom and jealousy, respectively. And because either of these problems can wreck a love affair, the one who's inconvenienced more may come up with plenty of "reasons" to leave the relationship.

Excuses will typically deny the true sexual cause.

But don't wait until you hear, or give, those excuses. Here's how you can help to save your love relationship when there's a charisma mismatch.

+ If you're the *Un-Def,* turn up your sexiness. Dress well and make an effort to think about sex more than you normally would.
+ If you're the *Def,* commit to staying faithful. When tempted to do more than flirt, remember what initially attracted you to your mate. Character and talent are likely to grow stronger through the years, while sex appeal may dwindle. Therefore, this relationship could offer long-term happiness that you won't find in a relationship based mostly on charisma.

AURAS

Both innate charisma and real-life sexiness show in the sexual chakra, so go ahead and research them at aura-level.

Strong charisma has a distinctive quality. When reading auras, you can find out if your lover is a sexual manipulator, using charisma to further career or social standing.

Begin with your usual Preparation Process: Pay attention to your inner awareness, then Get Big and set an intention to learn the truth about this person. (For more details, see Page 25.)

Plug-into your lover's aura at the Attractiveness databank at the Sexual Chakra. Ask, "Is there anything special about his/her sexual charisma?" Possibilities include:

- An **extra-large** amount of sexual energy that shimmers or vibrates.
- Symbols like **hooks** can show up visually or empathically.
- Truth knowledge or inner hearing may tell you that this person uses **sexual power** consciously to manipulate others.
- Emotionally, you may sense that this person enjoys **grabbing attention** from strangers by flaunting sex appeal.

Sexual charisma differs from interest in romance. The key is a strong ego factor. It's like the difference between being an excellent cook vs. trying to impress others with one's reputation as a gourmet.

Make Yourself Sexier

Society tells us that sexiness depends upon having a certain type of body. Unless you've been living in a cave, you know what's considered ideal for your gender and sexual persuasion....

Well, now you can just forget it! Do you want to attract lovers because you're great at matching a social stereotype? Only the most superficial people will be satisfied with that. And people like *that* don't read books like *this*.

Automatically, by reading this book, you've been outed as a deep person. You care about authenticity, so learn some deeper ways to increase your sexual charisma to the point where it will consistently show in your aura. And then watch your life change. Talk about the Law of Attraction!

To make yourself sexier, start with your inner **self-talk.** Spend 10 or more minutes a day wishing to connect strongly with people on a sexual level. Visualize, fantasize, or role play. Aim to arouse, then control, people's sexual interest in order to enhance your career, increase your popularity, etc.

(Does the thought make you squirm? Then maybe you'd be better off *not* trying for this extra sexual charisma. It isn't required for happiness, you know.)

Next, focus on your **physical appearance.** Make it match your sexy new self-image.

In reality shows, like "What Not to Wear," a person receives expert help for that physical self and, invariably, concludes "Oh, my self-image is so different now."

These two aspects of life, self-image and physical appearance, have a reciprocal relationship. Change one and then you can change the other. Still, unless someone happens to hand you a credit card to the tune of $5,000, plus free services from expert stylists of various kinds, start with the self-talk.

Afterwards, educate yourself a bit more about how to put together your wardrobe. TV shows and magazines can teach you. Radical changes may not be needed but it will be important to pay close attention to how you dress.

Find tasteful but effective ways to show the world what you've got. And, of course, doing regular exercise wouldn't hurt, either.

But neither physical nor mental changes are going to succeed long-term unless you also construct sexier new thought forms. **Thought forms** are astral-level patterns that affect people subconsciously.

Resolve that from now on, before you go outside, you will pause and consult a mirror. Every time! No exceptions!

Adjust your physical appearance. The goal is to project sexiness. Check out your grooming and clothes. After every change that you make, fluff your hair (or lovingly pat your bald pate) and affirm out loud, "I'm sexy and desirable."

This way, you won't just be making surface improvements but you'll strengthen and reinforce a super-sexy thought form.

For this to work, you must consistently do this ritual each and every time that you prepare to go out in public, even if you're just walking the dog or going out to buy coffee. To build sexual charisma, you'll need to work on all three aspects every day: Inner, outer, plus building up that charismatic thought form.

And to make sure that your own aura doesn't contain STUFF that sabotages your efforts, invest in personal sessions as needed with a healer who has skills to help at that level. Otherwise, old cords of attachment, etc., can get in your way.

Yes, it's a major commitment, choosing to project an extra-intense sexuality. With consistent effort, you can have it. Nobody can stop you. And you'll enjoy the benefits.

Could there be a downside to this self-improvement project?

Building sexual charisma will take long-term effort, detracting from other aspects of your personal growth. Since one can only take on so many major projects at a time, skimping on other aspects of life is a price you must be willing to pay.

Also note: It will take additional practice to temper your sexual charisma with finesse, elegance, and confidence.

Alas, there's always the possibility that, if you don't fine-tune the nuances, you'll come across as phony or cheap. But do the job right and you can succeed. Lady Diana did.

Yet you may have even greater success by practicing self-acceptance.

- When God makes a *toaster*, does it have hub caps?
- Will a *radio* ever warm up a room like a *radiator?*

Whatever your natural level of sex appeal, it was installed in perfect proportion to your other strengths. Accept this and, long-term, you will be your most attractive, no games required.

6. Charm

Life's charmers—when you meet them at work, don't they make your 9-5 go faster? Teaming up with someone who is not merely competent but adorable, what a great way to have extra fun along with greater success!

In your love life, a playful, agreeable personality can keep your romance ever fresh.

But know what? A bright new sprig of hemlock can look mighty fresh, too.

BODY LANGUAGE

With any two people, the one who exudes more **physical confidence** tends to be the one with more charm. Comparing your charm versus your partner's, don't confuse confidence with **posture.** Confident body language can range from strongly commanding to elaborately casual. And some of the biggest slouchers you know exude immense confidence. Think Hugh Grant or John Cusack.

Nonverbal enticements can be subtle. For example, unlike animals who aggressively charge toward their prey, charmers lean in for the seduction.

When your knees start to wobble, wait before you trust a charmer with little things like your credit card or your private parts.

Observe this cutie in group situations. How much charm does he/she lavish on people other than you?

FACE READING

Dimples come in many varieties, each signaling a different type of charm. Read dimples on the left side of the face to learn about your

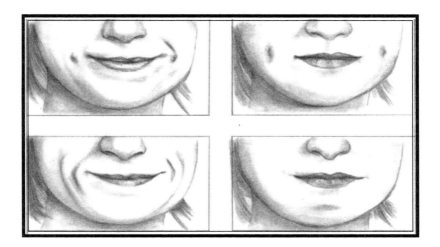

Illustration 8. DIMPLES

Dimples can be so charming, but they are NOT all created equal.

Become a Dimple Detective. Start by noticing whether or not the person is smiling. The presence or absence of a smile will place any dimples in the kind of context a face reader needs.

Half the drawings above show no smile, not even a fake one. See that?

Excellent! Now match the dimple type to its corresponding illustration:

+ No dimple
+ One peek a boo dimple
+ Powerline dimples
+ Permanent dimples

Just to spice things up, two of these illustrations show a type of wrinkle that can be mistaken for a dimple, but isn't. Can you spot that, too?

For answers, turn the page.

Illustration 8. QUIZ ANSWERS

PEEK A BOO DIMPLE	PEMANENT DIMPLES
Our smiler's one dimple shows on her right cheek, so she charms at work more than her social life.	Always charming, and probably very aware of the fact — don't trust this dimple owner until you have read her aura.
POWERLINE DIMPLES Two deep semi-circles grace the cheeks of the woman in this illustration. She has gained the kind of charm that relates to humility. But don't be jealous. Earning dimples like these is no fun. Life smashed her down; getting up, she choose gratitude.	**NO DIMPLE** Because no dimple shows here, all you know for sure from this one drawing is that this woman doesn't have permanent dimples. She might have one of the other types of dimple. To know for sure, you'll have to catch her smiling.

What about those **mouth-framer lines,** which you'll see in both our illustrations (Page 73) on the left? Don't confuse them with dimples.

Here's one way to tell the difference. Try smiling in front of a mirror. Now try, just try, to give yourself cheek dimples.

Well, trying won't work. You can't give yourself powerlines or peek a boos. If you have permanent dimples, you can't use your facial muscles to make those cute circles either appear or disappear.

But you *can* give yourself mouth-framer lines. Just scrunch up the corners of your mouth. (A fake smile helps, with lips closed, then pulled sideways.) What's the meaning, if lines like these show when you're *not* making faces in front of a mirror? This person habitually tries very hard to be pleasant… maybe too hard.

lover. Read dimples on the right side of the face to learn about someone at work.

Peek a boo dimples are circular shapes on cheeks that pop out with a smile, disappearing afterwards. Signaling a sweet disposition, these dimples reveal a talent for helping others to lighten up and laugh, especially when situations grow tense.

Permanent dimples are circular shapes on cheeks that show regardless of whether or not the rest of the face is smiling. Permanent dimples may signal a professional charmer, someone who knowingly manipulates others. Or this person may simply be chronically adorable. You be the judge.

Powerline dimples show with smiles, or become more pronounced with smiles, taking the form of a curvy, vertical crease (reminiscent of parentheses). Some cheeks develop multiple sets. With this kind of charm, the more, the better. Powerlines express habits like kindness, graciousness, and humility.

Charmingly Dangerous

The most dangerous kind of charm should be investigated when your partner is over 40. Does the face look 10 or more years younger than his/her real age? Observe carefully, because you may be responding to energy rather than the face itself.

Youthful energy is a plus, not so an overly youthful face. Consider yourself warned when a mature face shows no lines around the eyes or forehead, no softening at the jaws, no wrinkles anywhere.

That person is likely to be lighthearted and charming. Maybe he/she looks so youthful due to a healthy lifestyle. But it's equally possible that he/she hasn't aged facially because of arrested emotional development.

When sociopaths are in the news, notice how often they look younger than their years. What about psychologically healthy people? Being well adjusted but way self-absorbed, they may appear physically youthful, too. Cult members often look ultra-young, ascribing their winning appearance to the victorious powers of their "Move-ment." Maybe they're right but maybe they're not. Keep reading deeper.

What about today's social ideal, youthfulness via cosmetic surgery? Multiple face lifts and other surgical procedures have inner consequences.

Because of the reciprocal relationship between inner person and physical face, surgically reclaimed youthfulness does affect the inner person. The sort of procedures that cause movie stars to look half their age — we've been trained to think of this as a kind of "freshening up."

How crazy is that? You freshen up by using soap and water, not a knife.

What is the inner cost of an artificially extended shelf life? Reading auras, you can find out. Maybe there is no inner cost. Maybe the surgery brings inner youthfulness, dazzle, and a new start on life. Depends on the individual, doesn't it?

But before you go on to the level of auras, be honest with yourself. What is your motivation to be in this relationship? Do you seek a companion whose main value lies in helping you to feel important?

Perhaps you are seeking a trophy in human form. Many people do, and there is no law against it.

In this case, you might not want to read any deeper than you have so far. You want charm? And you have found it? Enjoy yourself!

But if you are curious to know more, aura reading would be a really smart choice.

AURAS

Charm shows so clearly in auras. It can be as fresh and pure as homemade ice cream. Unfortunately, some charmers have auras with hooks, pushiness, grease or other problems—not tasty additions to an ice cream sundae and unlikely to add to your happiness, either.

How can you tell what's going on?

Begin with your usual Preparation Process: Pay attention to your inner awareness, then Get Big and set an intention to learn about charm. (For more details, see Page 25.)

Plug-in at the Facades databank at the Communication Chakra. Ask: "What kind of charm is present here?" Whatever information you receive, make note.

Plug-in at the Intimacy databank at the Emotional Chakra. Ask: "What kind of charm is present here?" Whatever information you receive, make note.

Plug-in at the Spontaneity databank at the Sexual Chakra. Ask: "What kind of charm is present here?" Whatever information you receive, also make note.

Plug-in at the Presence When Entering the Room databank at the Physical Chakra. Ask: "What kind of charm is present here?" Whatever information you receive, make note.

Doing research like this, you will learn to recognize variations on the themes of charm.

Charm can be delicious. It can be sincere. Some of the most adorable people you'll meet have no idea at all how charming they are.

And when someone's natural behavior melts your heart, that's something more than charm. You haven't been either manipulated or merely amused. You have been blessed.

Every time a heart opens up more, the spiritual growth is lasting. And so, let's give three real cheers for those who possess authentic charm.

Still, it's caution time when the main thing you register about another person is "What a charmer!"

At such times, remember. Within the word "charm" lies "harm."

7. Competitiveness

Hope you never have to argue with a partner at work over which of you is less pushy. Who can win?

Having to defend yourself with a close friend — that might be worse.

But wait, there is something even more useless than either kind of argument: Long-term power struggles. To push this unpleasantness out of your future, take time in the present to compare how you and your partners handle competition.

BODY LANGUAGE

Every relationship has a "pecking order." Which of you is *one up?* Tell by interpreting gestures of dominance and submission. (See Page 105.)

Usually the pattern of a relationship will be set within the first encounter or two. Pay attention to what it can tell you.

FACE READING

Chin thrust can tell you a great deal about competitiveness. Read this face data in profile. Draw an imaginary line from the forehead to the chin (skip over the nose). During power struggles, victory typically goes to the warrior whose chin sticks out more.

Lip thrust also shows in profile. Do both lips stick out a little or a lot?

Big lip thrust corresponds to *verbal* aggression. The partner with more lip thrust will push harder to have the last word in an argument.

Finally, check out **lip dominance.** In profile, does one half of the mouth stick out more than the other?

+ If the *upper lip* has more thrust, the person's best verbal weapon is to discuss feelings, attempting to uncover insights.
+ If the *lower lip* has more thrust, fighting will emphasize facts alone. The other person's feelings will be negated.

AURAS

You could spend hours comparing how people compete at every chakra (e.g., intellectually, sexually). But if you are racing to get to the finish, go straight to one chakra databank in particular.

Begin with your usual Preparation Process: Pay attention to your inner awareness, then Get Big and set an intention to gain more wisdom. (For more details, see Page 25.)

Plug-in at the Invincibility databank in the Physical Chakra, at the base of the torso. Ask, "What happens to this person's physical presence when competing?"

A large showing here matters most.

It's also fascinating to ask follow-up questions, like "What strengths are available for competition?" and "How does he/she feel about competing with others?"

Now, be brave and do the very same research on yourself.

Summon Your Inner Winner

Everyone has gifts encoded in auras, remember? So if you find personal patterns about losing in life, you can move 'em out. Gifts of your soul will remain.

What if you're not sure what those gifts would be? Plug-into your Physical Chakra once again. Choose the Physical Power databank. Ask, "What gift shows in how I connect physically to life on earth?" Put what you find into words and, please, don't stint on the praise. Each human being was created with talent for becoming a winner.

8. Confidence

Confidence is one of those subtleties that can make or break a relationship. Ideally, you and your lover (or business associate) can boast similar amounts. Then you'll understand each another.

But what if, secretly, one of you possesses far less confidence? In an ideal world, the more confident partner would provide encouragement. In real life, alas, what happens when one partner suffers from a hidden lack of confidence? Eventually this may trigger the other partner's contempt.

Which way is it to be in your most prized relationships? For maximum confidence in a happy outcome, don't gamble without knowing the odds. Read people deeper right now.

BODY LANGUAGE

Reading confidence is one of the glories of body language.

To some degree, confidence is situational, rising or falling dependinig upon feedback from others in the conversation. **Posture** is the best way to read this changeable version of confidence:

+ From the *neck up,* does this person stand tall or slump?
+ How about *mid-range posture,* from neck to waist?
+ Don't forget to read *bottom-line posture,* all the way down through the pelvis, butt and legs. (Yes, be confident enough to take a quick stare.)

For deeper clues to confidence, scrutinize **tension around the eyes.**

+ When you talk to him/her, are the eyes *wide open* and relaxed? That's confidence.
+ A more defensive mindset shows when, mid-conversation, eyes *squint.*

+ Especially notice when the lower half of each eye, right next to the tear duct, tightens up. Tense *inner eye corners* show as extreme lack of confidence.

A completely different set of confidence data from body language relates to **eye gaze.** How does the other person meet your eyes? (Reading this on yourself, stand with your back to a mirror. Turn. Quickly catch your eyes in the mirror. Then freeze the position of facial muscles while you evaluate.)

+ Does eye contact seem *direct* and natural. Score extra points for confidence.
+ Lack of confidence can show in *averted* eyes, extra *blinking*, or eyes that *shift* around uneasily.
+ Does the person *glare* and stare, turning the eye contact into a staring contest? That could be way too much "confidence" for comfort.

Like you, I've heard that eyes reveal everything. Well, don't be so easily satisfied. That kind of "everything" doesn't really count for much. For instance, reading confidence at shoulders can tell you at least as much as all the aforementioned body language clues from eyes.

Shoulders symbolize handling responsibility. Is one held higher than the other?

+ For interpretation, consider that the *right* shoulder corresponds to a sense of duty regarding work.
+ The *left* shoulder reveals how your partner handles commitments in personal life.

After you read confidence as shown in shoulder position, also read the degree of **tension** in shoulders. No, you don't have to touch physically. Use your eyes, supplemented by imagination.

+ *Relaxed* shoulders convey a healthy degree of confidence.
+ *Sagging* shoulders reveal some degree of giving up.
+ *Hunched-up* shoulders suggest trying too hard, pushing to be confident or ultra-responsible.

Take Your Own Exit Poll

Political pollsters aren't the only ones who pay close attention to exits. Body language connoisseurs are very aware of how people enter or leave a scene. It reveals so much about confidence.

Does this person enter a scene like a champ or a loser?

Whatever happens during the interaction, a final symbolic display of confidence will be made at the end. Catch it. Take your nonverbal poll.

Sometimes you can even catch expression and posture during relatively private times. That would be either right before the person's grand entrance or else right after the official exit.

Confidence before and after joining the main group — what you spot may surprise you. Should you find secret insecurity, let it open up your heart of compassion.

Is it just coincidence that well-tailored suits mask shoulder data so well? You'll read shoulder language better when that suit jacket is off.

Finally, let's view one more body language category for reading confidence. **Hands** can supply quite the play-by-play commentary.

* *Hidden* in pockets or beneath a table, hands expose shyness.
* Clear *visibility* correlates with self-assurance.
* Displaying the *palms* shows the strongest possible confidence.
* What would score as *insecurity?* Telltale signs are hands tucked under crossed arms, a fingertip stroking the face or the mouth, nervously moving fingers.
* *Bitten fingernails,* of course, read like a billboard for low self-esteem.

+ What if the person positions hands with joined fingertips (sometimes known as *steepling* the hands)? This demonstrates confidence about his/her "superior" mind.

Can body language ever show too much confidence? Only the clueless will let outsiders see an arrogant swagger. Only the cocky will reveal a condescending sneer. So supplement your study of body language by reading yet deeper.

FACE READING

Teeth reveal life lessons around confidence. A *gap* between the front teeth suggests hidden insecurity. This may be covered up with jokes or bravado or spinach. But now you, the face reader, won't be so easily fooled.

A different problem arises when the *front teeth overlap* or cross each other, signifying inner conflict. If you have this pattern, it's as automatic a habit as grinding your teeth. You'll criticize yourself again and again.

But the habit can be broken. Patiently and persistently, pause the nasty self-talk. Then substitute praise. Surely you can find worthy things you've done, or personal qualities, that deserve to be valued.

Small front teeth also relate to confidence issues. Compare the size of the front teeth to the rest of the upper teeth; small front teeth are not much larger than their neighbors. They indicate natural humility.

By definition, people with this gift don't brag about it. Nor may they give themselves the full credit that they are due. As a face reader, never confuse humility with lack of confidence.

Large front teeth indicate a goodly share of personal ego, serving as a kind of confidence shield. Now there's an image to make it more fascinating when you brush your teeth!

Imagine, you're shining up the physical symbol of a good-sized ego, something that can really help with feeling confident.

What if the two middle teeth are way larger than the others? *Extra-large front teeth* suggest that self-confidence has been supersized.

Before you judge someone who has this attribute, hold on. Maybe this soul needed a big ego because an extra-difficult life had been planned.

Still, when somebody in your life has whopper chompers for front teeth, be prepared to deal with a strong personality. Large chunks of willfulness may correspond to the full dental display. Personal confidence won't be lacking but humility might.

When Body Language Stinks

Yoicks! It's like having bad breath. Maybe worse, because even well meaning friends aren't likely to tell you if you've got... a body language problem.

Could you be offending people? More likely, you could be blocking your own happiness. One thing's for sure. When your body language sends a mixed message, nobody wins.

Mixed messages can (and do) happen in many ways. One example is if you say, "I'm so mad at you," but facially contradict the words by grinning. And although a confusing message like this is easy to give, living with the consequences isn't easy at all.

Consistently sending the wrong feedback can break your heart. For example, how effective will your words be if attempts to claim your power are accompanied by body language that says, "I'm defeated"?

Don't despair. Even the knottiest body language problem can be untangled. Begin by giving yourself — and the knot —some slack. As therapists say, "Stop blaming the victim."

- Maybe you saw the wrong movies.
- Maybe you grew up with a lousy role model for nonverbal communication.
- Shame on that hamster from your childhood who couldn't teach you effective ways to communicate!

Seriously, whatever happened in the past, your time of power is now. Take advantage of it by learning how to send **congruent messages**. Once you've practiced, it's no harder than matching your socks to your shirt.

First, write down a variety of statements to practice with, like, "I feel really happy," "What you're doing makes me furious," and "You hurt my feelings."

Practice saying one statement at a time. Stand near a mirror but don't look at your reflection. Not yet!

Speak ultra expressively, as though you were auditioning for the starring role in a movie. Repeat your performance three times. Then freeze. Pivot toward the mirror and inspect your body language.

What does the mirror show about your face and body? Try to look objectively.

If you were photographed right now, what would the caption be, based on body language alone?

For even better coaching, invite a friend with good social skills to join you at the mirror and give feedback. That friend could also snap photos of you or, for super-deluxe coaching, videotape your performance. Compare your facial reality show to the script that you meant to communicate. Ouch?

Mixed messages may cover up fear of expressing certain feelings. Discuss problems with your friend or do whatever else it takes to clear up patterns that sabotage your body language. You have the right to feel, and show, the full range of human emotions.

AURAS

Confidence issues can show beneath ramrod posture or the mightiest set of front teeth. The only way to know for sure about confidence, here and now, is to read at the deepest level, auras.

Begin to investigate by doing your usual Preparation Process: Pay attention to your inner awareness, then Get Big and set an intention to open your heart. (For more details, see Page 25.)

Then plug-in at the Confidence databank at the Power Chakra and ask: "What happens when he/she needs self-confidence?"

Strengths may inspire you. But many people show a depressingly huge amount of STUFF in this databank. (Except, wait. Remember? STUFF can always be healed.)

Before STUFF is healed, how would confidence problems show? Think of times when you were in school, taking a big test in your worst subject. Those "butterflies in the stomach" flew around in your solar plexus chakra. Some little butterflies! Maybe each one felt like it weighed a ton.

So that's why you've been researching at the Power Chakra, located in the pit — or chasm — of your stomach.

If a co-worker or lover has confidence issues, offer gentle support.

If you're the one with those inner wobblies, start by healing past pain. Work your way up to the present. Or vice versa.

Who cares which order you choose, past-to-present or present, then past? You do, because you're the one with the power. Choose the way that you want to heal.

"Victim" is such a popular word. Yet no matter how horrible someone's ordeal, further victimization is *optional*.

Each person is responsible for his/her own self-confidence. And, thank goodness, that can be so much easier to develop than abs of steel.

9. Conflict

Choose an important work relationship in your life right now. How much conflict can you reasonably expect from it? You don't know yet, do you? So educate yourself here and now. You might consider this category of reading people to be a form of career insurance.

Romantics, don't skip this section, either. Lovey-dovey though you may be during the courtship stage, eventually you're gonna have to deal with conflict. Will that bring you to your knees... or to the exit door? Even worse, will you morph into a door*mat*? Not if you know and respect how both of you handle conflict, so read on.

BODY LANGUAGE

Body language isn't as good as aura reading for predicting if there will be conflict. But should you get into an argument, it's useful to compare each person's **gesture range.** Arms, head and face will all be revealing.

+ Gestures that *expand* (compared to normal gesture size) mean that a person isn't afraid to confront you.
+ Gestures that *contract*, or stiffen, expose a different pattern: anger expressed through withdrawal.

Know your style. Don't assume that your partner's style is like yours. For more help related to this, turn to "10 Rules to Fight Fair," Page 92.

FACE READING

Jaw width reveals how conflict affects you and others *inwardly*, so check out those hinges.

+ *Narrow jaws* mean an Early Detection Warning System. With this, you'll be the first in a relationship to recognize conflict. You also have the requisite courage to initiate discussion about the problem.

If you have this talent, use it. Either fix a conflict or get out of the relationship. Otherwise, you'll suffer enormously. Long-term conflict could even make you physically ill.

+ *Wide jaws* suggest that you're well adapted to handling conflict. You may even revel in it... being stubborn to the core.

+ Most people have *moderate jaw width*. If your jaws qualify, look out for others at either extreme. Otherwise, their behavior can blindside you.

Chin thrust is another facial characteristic related to conflict style. When you fight with someone, the person with the bigger chin thrust is likely to win.

So pull out your mirror right now, and soon as you can do a discrete check on others, take a look at that profile.

+ *Out-angled chins* correspond to a strong response.

+ *In-angled chins* (sometimes called "receding") go with compassionate conflict resolution, the intent to make each situation win-win for everyone concerned.

+ *Even chin thrust* suggests mastery of force. When push comes to shove, that push will be only as strong as warranted by the situation.

AURAS

Hidden conflict can ripple through anyone's energy field. Why should that be any of your business? That person's long-term conflict patterns will eventually be projected onto *you*.

The imbalance won't be as obvious as, say, Gollum's split personality in "The Two Towers." But what you don't know still can hurt you. So do research now into your partner's Warrior Style databank.

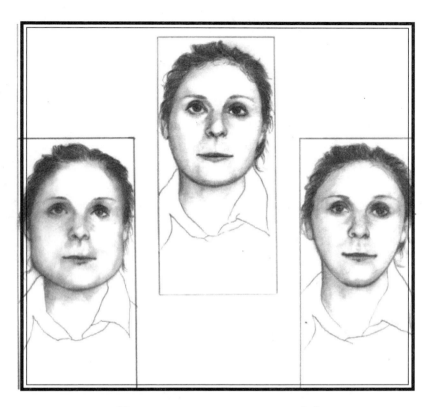

Illustration 9. Jaw Width

Reading jaws as a physiognomist, keep it simple. Find that hinge-place on either side of the head, located just a bit higher than the mouth. Whether those jaws are lean, muscular, flabby or bony, let's just focus on width.

+ Find the widest part, then consider. Is this wide in proportion with the rest of the face?
+ Which illustration is narrowest?
+ Which widest?
+ Which illustration shows the most moderate jaw width?

To find answers, turn the page.

Begin with your usual Preparation Process: Pay attention to your inner awareness, then Get Big and set an intention to learn about this person's way of being. (For more details, see Page 25.)

Plug-in at the Power Chakra and ask, "How does this person handle conflict?" (Or be fancy and ask, "What is this person's style as a warrior?")

Accept whatever information you receive.

Illustration 9. QUIZ ANSWERS

VERY WIDE JAWS	ALSO WIDE JAWS	AH, NARROW JAWS
Here's what shows in our first illustration: Very, extremely, unmistakably wide jaws.	"Wide," that's how I would describe the jaws shown in our middle illustration.	Here is your big contrast in this set of illustrations. The jaws here are narrow.
Really, could these jaws be any wider without making the pretty woman's head explode?	You were expecting this picture would show you moderate jaw width, but we tricked you, right? Start checking out jaws of the people around you and you will mostly find that people's jaws are less full than these.	Sometimes you'll see even narrower ones. (Those would count as Very Narrow Jaws.) Keep looking. (And while you're at it, regardless of your jaw width, no need to clench them tight while you concentrate, reading faces.)

Conflict can be held in any of the chakras, of course. So if you're interested in **anticipating** danger, read these additional databanks:

+ At the Root Chakra, in the Dealing with Reality databank, ask "How does this person handle problems in life?"
+ At the Sexual Chakra, in the Sexual Problem-Solving databank, ask "How does this person handle sexual conflicts?"
+ At the Power Chakra, in the Flexibility databank, ask "How does this person handle conflicts between his/her ideas and yours?"
+ At the Emotional Chakra, in the Conflict Resolution databank, ask "How does this person handle emotional conflicts?"
+ At the Communication Chakra, in the Powerspeak databank, ask "How does this person communicate when there's a conflict?"
+ At the Spiritual Chakra, in the Spiritual Growth databank, ask "How does this person handle belief systems that are different from his/her own?"
+ At the Soul Chakra, in the Authentic Choice databank, ask "Right now, does this person prefer to live in harmony or to live in conflict?"

Besides revealing where potential conflict is stored, aura reading can reveal a great deal about how a person **handles** conflict.

Is the conflict faced honestly? Or does the person have habits of denial, avoidance, irresponsibility, or the like?

To find out, while you're still plugged into any of the previous chakra, ask this follow-up question: "How does he/she avoid conflict?"

In the databanks I have invited you to research, **terrorists** typically carry intense patterns of conflict and hatred. So do other dangerous people.

If you discover that a person has this kind of STUFF going on, get as far away as you can. Go as fast as you can.

Do this without calling attention to yourself or otherwise creating drama.

---

10 Rules to Fight Fair

Even wars have rules. See if you and your partner can agree on these 10 rules to fight fair.

1. *When* **both** *of you are angry, don't fight. Sure, it might sound silly to make an appointment to argue but better to sound silly than to do the verbal equivalent of drag racing.*

2. *Take* **turns** *telling your side of the story. Whatever bothers you, don't be ashamed of it. You feel what you feel. Tactfully communicate the part you need to tell.*
   - *Try the time-honored formula: "When you do x, I feel y. Next time, would you please do z?"*
   - *For example, "When you make me go out to sushi bars, it makes me angry. I don't think that a requirement for dating you should be my willingness to eat raw fish. Next time, could I get to choose the restaurant?"*

3. *In a fair fight, both you and your partner must* **listen** *to each other.*
   - *In fact, to resolve the argument extra fast, take turns reflecting back the main points, one at a time, e.g., "So you're saying it makes you angry when I ask you to eat sushi?" Repeat what you've heard, calmly and sympathetically, to convince your partner that you're really listening.*

4. *Avoid* **blaming.** *Describe what has upset you without putting an edge to your words.*

● *For example, how effective would it be to tell your partner: "Smart people love sushi. Besides, your taste in food is so booooooooring."*

5. *Which brings us to this all-important rule: Avoid saying things that will* **hurt**. *In the energy of rage, it's tempting to lash out. Resist that temptation.*

● *Hurtful words are more "forever" than diamonds. If necessary, carry a band-aid to put over your mouth.*

6. *If the anger level escalates, go out and* **take a walk** *alone for 10 minutes.*

● *After calming down, you can make contact with the softer feelings underlying your anger, like hurt and worry. Beneath most arguments, each person has a vulnerability. Once you find yours, you won't be tempted to hide it by acting tougher than necessary.*

7. *Don't discuss past history. Be specific about what bothers you* **now**. *Anything else constitutes hitting below the belt, something that should be avoided (especially if your future plans with this person include having* **fun** *below the belt).*

8. **Apologize** *as appropriate. Incidentally, neither of you is allowed to get away with that patronizing cop-out, "I'm sorry that you feel blah-blah," as in, "I'm sorry that you feel personally attacked just because I like to eat conger eel."*

9. *Take a tip from the great relationship expert John Gray: For a man, complain about who a man* **is**, *not what he does. For a woman, ask her to change her* **actions**, *not who she is.*

10. *Treat every argument as a chance to* **fine-tune** *your relationship. Both of you can offer ideas about what would solve a problem.*

● *As you work out a solution, both of you will become more physically relaxed. Count this body language as proof positive that you have been fighting fair.*

10. Conformity

When you are with a group, how important is fitting in?

Trick question! Any answer is fine… unless you and your partner disagree.

Conformity mismatches can wreck a relationship. Prevent problems by learning about your differences.

It is, of course, entirely possible that reading your conformity styles will bring nothing but encouragement. Could the two of you be like peas in a pod-nership?

BODY LANGUAGE

Conformity leanings show in very obvious **physical leanings.** Let's say the two of you are partying at a friend's house. Do you and your special friend lean *toward* the group or *away?*

Next, explore the subtleties.

+ Do your *hands* point toward the crowd or away?
+ How about your *feet?*
+ Does one of you position *arms* or *legs* like the non-verbal equivalent of a "Keep out" sign?

How about **stress** related to being with the group? Does your partner physically relax, suggesting that he/she feels at home? Posture may turn rigid with disdain, discomfort, or discombobulation.

Head movements also reveal a person's comfort with conformity. A head cocked to one side indicates more interest than a head rigidly centered. Nods and an engaged expression also suggest that your partner is getting along with the group.

Did you know? Nonverbally, even the most sedentary group engages in a dance. Moving your head less than the others in your group constitutes being a wallflower.

In fact, one of the most intriguing ways to spot a nonconformist involves what is called **"interactional synchrony."**

That's a fancy term for "Why can't you just get along?" Only you're not observing fistfights, just background body language.

In any group, there's a beat in the background, even when no music plays. By watching videotapes of people in crowds, body language experts have discovered that one group member will always act as a kind of unofficial conductor, setting a background rhythm. Everyone else around unconsciously follows this leader, adding their own cute head nods, fidgets and the like.

Interactional synchrony includes behavior with silence. How long will people in the group wait to speak after the last one speaks?

Also, within one person's speaking, how long are the mini-silences between words and sentences? When you pay attention to a group's rhythms, it's fascinating how much you can learn.

For one thing, you'll find that nonconformists literally do march to the beat of a different drummer.

FACE READING

Ears are such rich sources of information, they're worth hunting for beneath hairstyles. To read conformity, focus on **ear angle,** how far the ear sticks out from the head. Observe from the front. Innies barely show, while outies spring forth like tree branches.

- Many ears negotiate a compromise, their *moderate angling* neither strongly in nor drastically out. (See Page 56, top two drawings, the right ear only). For compatibility, this is a gift. It suggests that you can get along with either of the ear-angle extremes. Now, what about those extremes?
- *In-angled ears* correspond to social conformity. (See Page 99, bottom drawings, left ear only.) Here's someone who'd prefer to belong to the group, any group. For an innie, good manners are instinctive.

+ *Out-angled ears* mark a born non-conformist, someone who'll either question the group's unspoken rules or dismiss them entirely. (See Page 56, top two drawings, the left ear only).

Whatever a person's conformity style, don't expect it to change any time soon. How can innies and outies avoid making each other squirm? Either laugh at your differences or choose to learn from them.

AURAS

Inner pain can distort a person's natural conformity style, and the best place to tell what's cooking deep down is... the oven.

No? Okay, you guessed it. Unless your friend or co-worker is an appliance, a better place for detective work would be his/her aura.

Spunky nonconformity becomes embarrassing when the independence hides stored-up anger. And gracious manners turn stifling when, secretly, some parts of a person are aurically half-dead.

So take the precaution of checking out all the relevant databanks. It's no big deal for auras to reveal *stress-built barriers* of one sort or another. You know what they say about inner healing. "When there's a wall, there's a way."

To protect yourself from surprises in the conformity department, investigate your partner's aura for major STUFF in the databanks of your choice. Begin with your usual Preparation Process: Pay attention to your inner awareness, then Get Big and set an intention to gain clarity about this person. (For more details, see Page 25 about how to do the technique.) Then go ahead and read these different Conformity databanks:

+ At the Physical Chakra, ask "How does he/she handle other people's rules?"
+ At the Power Chakra, ask "How open is he/she to other people's expectations?"

+ At the Spirituality Chakra, ask "How do other people's rules help him/her to evolve spiritually?"
+ At the Sexual Chakra, ask "How do other people's expectations empact his/her libido?"

Committing to a Love Relationship

Pop culture tells us that good sex is all the reason you need to commit to a love relationship.

If you're 18 years old, fine.

Otherwise, you can do better. Read a lover's aura before you commit to the relationship. Or else read that aura now and re-commit. Or not.

It really is smart to learn about your lover, in depth and detail. You don't have to know everything but, for the sake of a happy future, you do need to know about more than sex.

In this chapter, we have been exploring conformity issues. When you commit to a love relationship, you'll be dealing with your lover's personal style in every aspect of life. And he/she will be dealing with yours. There is a deep kind of conformity to which you both will be invited.

Any time you that have sex, even casual sex, **your aura will be connected to your lover's for the next three days.** Particles of one in the other, dancing away, filling each other's auric nooks and crannies. Yes, I'd call that a certain kind of conformity, wouldn't you?

A couple can work through any conformity problem, provided that both are willing to learn about each other, accept each other, and be patient. Model how that can be done!

For incentive, ask yourself this. Is there any sweeter conformity than that of long-time couples? Do your relationship right, and nobody else in the world will know so well how to please you.

11. Control

It could happen to you, the more easygoing half of a relationship. Bossiness was never an issue, not until the day you discovered that your partner was a control freak.

Outside of horror movies, Frankenstein monsters aren't easy to spot. Yet you can find them with deeper perception. And nobody, not even the suave-est, sneakiest control freak, has the power to keep you from learning the truth.

BODY LANGUAGE

Note the person's **gesture level** in front of the body. Are the majority of hand movements positioned at the solar plexus? That corresponds to a strong interest in leadership — or domination.

Need for control also shows in **personal grooming.** An ultra-neat appearance corresponds to guess what?

Just for fun, see how much you can learn about control needs from a person's choice of clothing.

+ People with a strong need for control often dress in tailored clothing.
+ They may like clothes to be carefully coordinated. Everything must match.
+ A preference for leather or other animal skins can be related to the need to dominate.
+ Some controlling personalities like fabrics with repeating small patterns.
+ Others just demand that clothes be perfectly clean and absolutely wrinkle-free.
+ Greater flexibility is revealed in clothes that flow, soft-textured fabrics and fabrics with abstract or floral patterns.

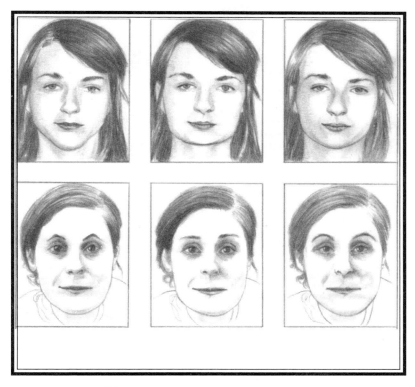

Illustration 10. SHAPES

Curved, straight, or angled — these are the three significant shapes to a face reader. So, first, understand the meaning of each shape.

+ Curved = Based on emotion
+ Straight = Related to using the mind
+ Angled = Emphasizing the need to control

Then add the meaning of the face category, such as:

+ Eyebrow shape = Framework for everyday thinking
+ Chin bottom shape = Basis for making decisions

Let's not forget the most important part. Before you combine those meanings, better make sure you can *see* them. Who here has which shape on eyebrows, on chin? Turn the page for answers.

FACE READING

Two parts of the face reveal a habitual need for control. **Eyebrow shape** discloses thinking patterns.

Angled eyebrows (which hinge somewhere along the top edge of the brow) correspond to intellectual detachment. Here's an independent thinker, someone who refuses to go along with anyone else's explanations or priorities. Spell that either "Fascinating" or "Trouble."

Next, turn to the shape of **chin bottoms.** *Angled* chin bottoms correspond to a will of iron. So does an angled beard bottom, like a goatee. (Learn more about chin bottom shapes at Page 110.)

Sometimes that strong will is just a way to balance out great sensitivity, as shown elsewhere in the face.

Regardless, you can expect the owner of an angled chin to make decisions with a "Me first" attitude. The more you try to boss around Mr. or Ms. Angled Chin, the more resistance you'll meet. That goes double for the proud wearer of a goatee.

Illustration 10. QUIZ ANSWERS

R. Eyebrow: Angled L Eyebrow: Straight Chin: Angled She's more controlling at work! But even socially, she really, really needs to get her way.	**Eyebrows: Curved Chin: Straight** Emotional IQ is high when she thinks. But acting, she cares more about principle than pleasing people.	**Eyebrows: Angled Chin: Curved** Managerial thinking is combined with the choices of a softie.
Eyebrows: Angled Chin: Straight She thinks like a manager, socially or at work. However, she bases her choices on principle.	**Eyebrows: Straight Chin: Curved** She thinks objectively, makes choices subjectively.	**Eyebrows: Curved Chin: Angled** Emotions rule when she thinks, but beware! When she takes action, what matters most is staying in control.

AURAS

Control patterns are most likely to show in the Power Chakra. Begin with your usual Preparation Process: Pay attention to your inner awareness, then Get Big and set an intention to learn in a balanced way about this person. (For more details, see Page 25.)

- If you're investigating a *work* relationship, choose the Power in Work Relationships databank and ask "Does he/she try to control other people at work?"
- Or if it's a *personal* relationship you're researching, plug-in at the Power in Intimate Relationships databank and ask: "Does he/she try to control the people he/she is close to?"
- Finally, plug-in at the Give Others Space databank at the Spiritual Chakra and ask "Does he/she tend to use psychic coercion?"

Win By Letting Go

What if, despite all precautions, you find yourself pulled into a battle with a controlling partner?

Handle it like a clever puzzle from the Orient that I'll bet you've seen. It's a colorful tube of woven straw into which you insert both thumbs. The harder you pull, the worse you stay stuck. To release, you must move in the **opposite** *direction, relaxing your thumbs.*

When somebody tries to control you, don't compromise your self-respect. But, for minor issues, remember that toy. Treat the "big deal battle" like a game. By seeming to let go, you'll win.

---

12. Criticism

Although critical people may be loveable, they're not always easy to love. Destructive, negative comments can wring the joy out of life... unless you develop a pretty dry wit yourself.

Reading your partner won't remove the tendency to criticize. But if you find it, at least you'll be prepared.

BODY LANGUAGE

Your first cue about criticism comes in **the set of a mouth,** when the face is relaxed. Tightness indicates fault finding, while pursed lips show fussiness. Relaxed lips are your ally.

Take a deep breath when you see a person's arms crossed in front of the chest. This **self-protective gesture** often precedes criticism.

All of us have moments when we feel defensive. It's something else to wear a defensive stance as routinely as underwear. If you tend to choose relationships with people who are chronically critical, ask yourself, "What's in it for me?"

FACE READING

Which people have a natural gift for criticism? They have **close-set eyes.** Physically, that means eyes that are less than one eye-width apart.

Can a person have just one close-set eye? Definitely. The other eye could have average set or even be far-set. For work relationships, just read the right eye. For personal relationships, read the left eye.

Where you find a close-set eye, there's a gift for paying close attention. Rejoice if your partner possesses this talent. It can pay off in career success, to mention doing meticulous work around the house.

But, yes, be aware of the potential challenge. Criticism may also be meticulous. Therefore, it's wise to discourage gossip or other negative conversations.

Reading people for criticism, you might also want to check your partner for **down-angled eyes.** Physically, this means that *outer* corners are lower than *inner* corners.

Again, read only the eye that pertains to your purpose, right for work partnership and left for personal relationship.

A down-angled eye signifies a problem-solving orientation. This can bring you many benefits, but the disadvantage is how often he/she may focus on problems. Resulting conversations may be about as welcome as having your cat present you with a dead mouse.

Keep in mind that eyes develop a down-angle after prolonged periods of suffering. (In Japan, they're called "weeping eyes.") Consequently, your critical friend may have a hugely compassionate heart.

Of course, patterns of criticism can be changed. So if you're the one with these patterns, move them out!

Not only is behavior shaped by free will but, over time, free will may change your face physically, too. A down-angled eye *can* turn up-angled. (I know because this has happened to me.)

Although eye set isn't as likely as eye angle to change physically, a person's efforts to compensate will cause him/her to develop a physical sign of affability: Wrinkles that fan out from the outer corners of the eye.

Most people call them "crow's feet" but I'm not inspired by the notion of using a human face as a place for animal tracks, so I prefer to use a different technical term for these wrinkles: **"Eye extenders."**

AURAS

Investigating criticism, are you? Don't try too hard!

Begin with your usual Preparation Process: Pay attention to your inner awareness, then Get Big and set an intention to open your heart and mind. (For more details, see Page 25.)

Then plug into the Tolerance databank at the Emotional Chakra and ask, "How does this person handle imperfection?"

Should critical patterns show up, be especially wary of armoring or other forms of hostility that you find in the aura. These can jeopardize your relationship.

(But do remember, please, that problems like these are reversible. STUFF is what gives an edge to an observant person's observations. And STUFF can always be healed.)

Also pay attention to what happens to a person's aura *during* a rant. If criticizing people makes his/her Power Chakra or Sexual Chakra grow bigger, you could be dealing with a sadist.

What if *you're* the one with the critical tendencies? Do what you can to lighten up.

Failing that, keep your gripes to yourself. Even "constructive" criticism may not be as helpful as you suppose.

Do the Math

In a love relationship, use the power of math to beat criticism.

Push yourself to find things to genuinely admire about your sweetheart. If you can keep the ratio of praise to criticism at 2:1, you're more likely to live as a two-some instead of a lone-some.

13. Decision Making

How much fun is it to hike with gravel in your shoes? Similar discomfort can develop when your partner's decision-making style is a drag. Find out where both of you stand.

BODY LANGUAGE

Even when you and your partner must make decisions about something simple, your relationship dynamics may not be simple at all. Within your first few meetings, the two of you have established complex **deference patterns**.

Operating at a subconscious level, these patterns come into play whenever two or more people make choices together. Body language can help you to understand the dynamics, especially if you use multiple senses to investigate. In the office, the kitchen, the bedroom… which one of you tends to make the decisions?

+ After your **eyes** have locked in a power struggle, who turns away first?
+ Is it possible to hear **deference** in a voice? Sure! Listen for a voice that fades away hesitantly at the end of a sentence, becoming quieter or dropping in pitch.
+ Is it possible to hear **dominance** in a voice? Dominant speech is extra strong at the final words, be it voice volume or speed or emphasis or, suddenly, extra-precise enunciation.
+ **Vocal quality** matters more than which of you has the last word. (This is a great example of how body language can trump surface appearances.)
+ Power dynamics move like a dance, a tricky one. So learn to read the **vertical** element. At decision-making time, does one partner slump or stoop? Or does one of you stand straighter than normal?

Avoid These Three Decision Busters

Whatever you've learned so far about decision making in your relationship could be upsetting. Perhaps you feel so disgusted that you're like, "Enough is enough. It's time to quit."

But don't. At least, don't quit before you learn from the experience. Otherwise you're doomed to repeat the same pattern.

What can you do when body language shows that the balance of power in your relationship is just plain lousy?

● Maybe you're tired of being pushed around, never getting what you want.

● Maybe you hate feeling passive and figure that a different lover or boss would bring out the best in you.

● You could even be sick and tired of constantly winning. Victory can feel hollow. Besides, how can you respect a person who defers to you constantly?

None of this has to be. It helps to avoid these three traps.

DECISION BUSTER #1: *"I need space"*
Moving away from your relationship, taking a vacation, finding a new place to live... You can sum up the spacey approach to problem solving with one word: Excuse.

Unless you can find somewhere to move where **you** will not have to be present, space can't really solve your problems.

But what if you can't think on your own because the other person is too oppressive?

You don't need space. You need strength. Resolve to find it and use it.

DECISION BUSTER #2: *"I need time"*
Time heals all wounds, they say. Death could heal your wounds, too. Yet waiting for time (or death) is a rather passive form of healing. It could take years... and may never teach you much.

I do feel your pain. For instance, it's scary and hurtful if you *must deal with a bully at work. You know very well that you will need to learn from this bully if you want your next job to be any better. With all respect, waiting for time to fix your problems is just plain lazy.*

DECISION BUSTER #3: *"I don't know"*
Why not? Whatever keeps you from taking responsibility for your own choices — that's something you can choose to heal.

Until then, indecision will transfer from one relationship to another. That includes coping patterns learned way back in childhoods. Cords of attachment to childhood pain can bombard you with toxic energy 24/7. If you feel stuck in the past, there's good reason.

But you are stronger than any old patterns and you **can** *decide to change them. Even a longstanding, painful pattern can become history, provided that you choose to heal. If you can't do it on your own, quit saying "I don't know" and try saying "Help!"*

Professional help comes in many forms. Don't go back to approaches that didn't work for you in the past. Explore new approaches, including the jet-propelled technologies of the new millennium:

● **Energy Medicine** *uses your physical body as the point of entry for healing your aura.*

● **Energy Psychology** *uses emotions as the point of entry.*

● **Energy Spirituality** *use your aura itself as the point of entry. (This kind of healing includes professional techniques to permanently cut toxic cords of attachment.)*

● **Hypnosis,** *today, is a sophisticated and well-researched tool for using your inner Wise Mind for permanent healing.*
You can learn more about all these technologies. Google away! Then trust your judgment. Which sort of therapy would suit you best? You do know.

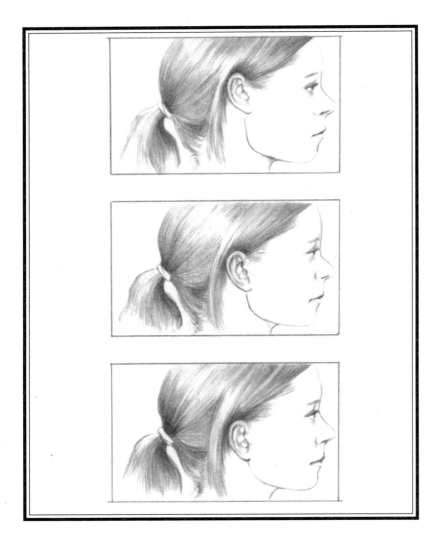

Illustration 11. EAR POSITION

High, low, and **middle** are our choices for ear position. What have we here? (Really look. Set expectations aside.) Turn the page for answers.

FACE READING

Educate yourself about **values** that underlie decisions by reading the shape at **chin bottoms.** (See the illustration on Page 99.)

+ A *curved* chin relates to making decisions based on people's feelings.
+ A *straight* chin relates to decisions based on principle.
+ An *angled* chin alerts you that the need to stay in control motivates decisions.

In addition, everyone has a favorite **timing** for making decisions. It shows clearly to a face reader. Ignore this very personal trait at your peril. To begin, you'll need a view in profile where the head is even, not tilting up or down.

Does the earlobe hangs *below* the nose tip? This constitutes low ear position. If, instead, the top of the ear shows *above* the eyebrow, that's high ear position.

Most ears hold to a middle position, located *between* the top of the eyebrow and the tip of the nose.

For work partnerships, read the position of the *right* ear. For love relationships, read the *left* ear.

And for either ear, double check that the head position really is level before you read. Tilting a head upwards will make any ear appear low. Always read faces on the level, another person's face or your own face in *two* mirrors (which you will need to see ear position). See photos on the level. Hold this book on the level, too.

Okay, back at ear position, contrasting extremes can strain a relationship until you allow for differences:

+ With *low* ears, you need plenty of time to make choices. Soundness of decisions increases, along with your comfort level, when you can gather lots of information and evaluate it carefully. Your potential challenge is needing so much time.

Illustration 11. QUIZ ANSWERS

Well, well, well, what have we here?

Reading ear position, let's think outside the box. Then let's add some lines. Normally you'd make these lines imaginary, not inked-in. Either way, "draw" parallel lines at the lowest parts of the eyebrow and nose. This helps you to read this tricky face category accurately.

Yes, this counts as a **high** ear, but barely. For practical purposes, when a face trait is this close to a toss-up, I would just skip it and read something else that shows more clearly.

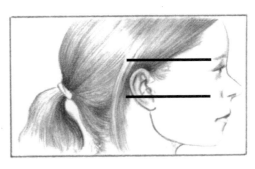

Now this is a **low** ear. How satisfying, even if it isn't what you, perhaps, expected when you first saw this set of drawings. (Imagining, can you move her ear up to **middle** position?)

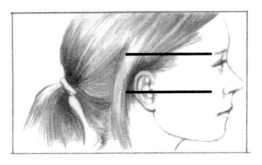

Adding our lines, this low ear seems **very low.** But I can assure you that I have read plenty of ones this low. Some ears are even lower. Keep reading faces and you'll find them, too.

- With *high* ears, you make your best decisions quickly, intuitively. When your partner takes longer, it can cause acute discomfort. You need closure. Your potential challenge is impulsiveness.
- Anyone whose ear position lies right in the middle can be ultra-flexible about the pace for making choices. But your potential challenge is a lack of tolerance for the rest of humanity — judging those who seem too slow or too fast, compared with your "perfect" timing.

Is any of these ways superior? Of course not. All the more reason to honor the natural rhythms belonging to you and your partner!

AURAS

Aw, "decision" can be just another name for agony. Is this the case for your partner? Find out by reading the relevant databank.

Begin with your usual Preparation Process: Pay attention to your inner awareness, then Get Big and set an intention to learn about your partner. (For more details, see Page 25.)

Plug-in at the Decision-Making databank in the Power Chakra. Ask, "How does he/she make decisions?"

Indecisiveness means that old problems distort your partner's natural gifts (such as face data about ears and chins). Once STUFF is released, gifts will flow.

But not all indecisiveness relates to problems. For instance, the Decision-Making databank could reveal a talent for seeing multiple points of view, a talent that will remain long after self-doubt has been overcome.

Knowing about gifts of the soul can help you to be supportive of your partner.

Be sure to check out your own gifts, too. It will make you more optimistic about the outcome of your own journey here at Earth School.

14. Earthiness

How down-to-earth is your partner? How earthy are you, for that matter? This quality doesn't make people superior, so don't worry about yourself either way. But do pay attention. Compare your earthiness to that of your partner at work or in your personal life.

Why? Similarity brings respect and, even, lasting compatibility.

Knowing about your different tendencies can also help you to bond as opposites, one of you a better teacher about this funky place called "Earth School."

What doesn't work is lack of truth in advertising, like someone who claims to be down-to-earth but really isn't.

Earthiness helps a person to be realistic, also sensuous, street-smart, pragmatic, responsible with money and commitments.

Self-description is pitifully unreliable as a way to gauge earthiness. Does your partner has feet of bedrock or clay? Find out.

BODY LANGUAGE

Your single best clue to earthiness from body language is **postural thrust.** What the heck is that? "Posture" includes moving muscles forward aggressively or leaving them slack. "Thrust" equals perky, propped up, sticking out, fully inflated, etc.

If you were born with talent as a physical empath, you can look at somebody's posture and *feel* how those muscles are being used to emphasize the anatomy. Where does the body seem most alive?

Besides that, you can definitely *see* postural thrust. Just look at him/her in profile. Imagine a straight line running from head to toe (if the person is standing) or from head to seat (if the person is sitting). Some part(s) will always lean forward compared to the rest.

Whether you see or feel, start by comparing the two lengthwise halves of the body. Then check out the body as a whole.

+ Emphasizing any part of the body from the *waist down* spells earthiness.
+ Slumping any part of the body from the *waist down* signals ambivalence or indifference. This could mean problems like chronic resentment, lack of ambition, laziness, depression, shame, or a disconnect from everyday reality.
+ Emphasizing any part of the body from the *waist up* reveals that another aspect of life matters more than earthiness, e.g., emotions, intellect or spirituality.
+ Slouching any part of the body from the *waist up* indicates a problem with self-confidence, emotional courage, spiritual connection, etc.
+ *Balanced* postural thrust suggests earthiness supported by a lively inner life.

Which form of postural thrust is best? That's like asking if vanilla ice cream beats chocolate. Maybe this partner will treat you to a flavor you never tried before. Respect that as part of his/her curriculum here at Earth School.

No matter what your partner emphasizes, you can work with it in your relationship.

Maybe you can even learn something that helps you to grow as a person.

Trust Your Thrust

Your own postural thrust may be different from what you assume. How can you read it accurately?

Next time you unexpectedly walk in front of a mirror, freeze from the shoulders down. Then turn your head and look.

As you read the above interpretations, don't be harsh, okay? Make the most of your personal brand of earthiness.

Illustration 12. PRIORITY AREAS

To read the three Priority Areas, compare these different lengths on a face:

+ Area I: The *intellectual area* extends from the hairline to the highest part of the eyebrows.
+ Area II: The *ambition area* reaches from the top of the eyebrows down to the lowest part of the nose.
+ Area III: The *grounding area* spans nose tip to chin bottom.

For each of these faces, which Priority Area is longest? And which face is the tricky one? Turn the page for answers.

FACE READING

To learn about earthiness as a long-term habit, read faces. Specifically, read **priority areas.** Wait until your partner's mouth is closed.
Then look on the level and compare the relative sizes of these three
face lengths.

+ Priority Area I: The *intellectual area* extends from the
  hairline to the highest part of the eyebrows.
+ Priority Area II: The *ambition area* goes from the top of
  eyebrows down to the lowest part of the nose.
+ Priority Area III: The *grounding area* reaches from that
  lowest part of the nose down to the chin bottom.

How can you tell which is longer? Some people see the difference
easily, just by paying attention. But I'm not one of these people, so I
have developed the two following methods.

+ My favorite method is to physically make a "ruler" by spread-
  ing my thumb and index finger. I'll hold this improvised
  ruler up against the person's face, in person, comparing
  priority areas. Or for a photo reading, I'll hold my "ruler"
  against parts of the photo. Either way, I'll measure each area
  in turn, moving my fingers to expand or contract the "ruler."
+ Another approach is to eyeball one priority area at a time,
  just focusing on how long it is, nothing else. Go on to the
  next, then the next. One section will *feel* longer or shorter
  than the others. (You may have to compare these three areas
  a few times to wake up your intuition for this kind of
  feeling.)

Now, what can priority areas tell you about earthiness?

Is Priority Area III the *longest,* or tied for first place? This signals a gift for earthiness, e.g., someone likely to give decent driving
directions.

Is Priority Area III *shortest?* Then your partner may grow bored
with physical pursuits. His/her true interests lie elsewhere.

What if you're not particularly earthy but you'd like to be? You could have a teensy weensy Priority Area III. But if you care a lot about earthiness, experiment by paying closer attention to physical life. Spend more time on it daily. In short, make it a... priority.

Then, guess what? Any priority area that you favor in life will physically grow longer compared to the others. Happened to Elvis! Over time, it can happen to you, too.

Incidentally, which gifts go with those other two priority areas? Area I longest signals an interest in *learning.* Area II longest reveals innate fascination with *ambition,* accomplishing things in life and then receiving credit.

Whichever aspect of life you favor habitually, your face will eventually shift long-term to show as your life priority.

So far you have learned how to find earthiness by reading face data and by examining that fun-to-watch body language I have dubbed "postural thrust,"

Reading your partner and/or yourself, you have found certain strengths. But keep in mind that living up to one's potential is different from just being talented.

What makes the difference? It's how much STUFF a person carries in his/her energy field. And nothing reveals STUFF more clearly than reading auras.

Illustration 12. QUIZ ANSWERS

PRIORITY AREA I dominates. Her personality emphasizes learning.	**PRIORITY AREA II** dominates. Her personality emphasizes getting results.
PRIORITY AREA III dominates. Her personality emphasizes earthiness.	Here's our tricky face with **EQUAL PRIORITY AREAS.** Multiple talents rule.

AURAS

One-stop shopping for earthiness is available at the Grounding databank at the **Physical Chakra**. Really earthy people come alive there, sending out a huge blast of energy.

Ultimately, anyone can project a large amount of energy at this databank. It isn't about priorities in life so much as fully being yourself. If you're in a human body, yes, you have your own magnificent way of being down-to-earth. Which shows more, gifts or STUFF?

To research, begin with your usual Preparation Process: Pay attention to your inner awareness, then Get Big and set an intention to learn from this person's way of being. (For more details, see Page 25.) Then plug-in at the Grounding databank and ask, "How grounded is this person?"

Trust what you get.

For extra nuance, go on to explore your partner's *kind* of earthiness. This involves each person's **version of reality.** Despite appearances, all human beings don't live on the same planet. Some inhabit a grim reality, while others live in a world of beauty and joy.

Wouldn't you like to know about your partner's kind of reality? Simple!

While you're still plugged into the Physical Chakra, ask this follow-up question: "What kind of a world does he/she live in?"

For a *work relationship,* your comparison has practical implications. To assess work projects, like dealing with a new client, trust the partner who is earthier. For "the vision thing," give extra credit to the one who's less earthy.

In a *love relationship,* it's easiest if your styles of earthiness are similar. Often, however, one partner squeaks like a piccolo but the other booms like a tuba.

How can you make beautiful music together? All instruments can harmonize. Don't blame your lover for sounding different from you.

15. Embarrassment

Read people deeper to predict potential embarrassment... and to protect yourself from unwittingly sabotaging a valued relationship.

BODY LANGUAGE

Body language is your best way to predict (and prevent) **sexual embarrassment. Eye gaze** is the category that matters.

Ever feel like you're on the *receiving* end of crude advances? Chances are, you're not just imagining it. Someone who comes on too strong for your taste is previewing future incompatibility—either sexually or socially or both.

No, you're not weird to mind if your partner comes on too strong. It's rude to indulge in prolonged stares at a man's crotch, a woman's breasts or anybody's butt. Even furtive glances won't go unnoticed by the recipient, since each of us has an instinctive sexual radar.

How about *causing* embarrassment, rather than receiving it? Strong attraction can trip you up unless you moderate your come-hither signals. Pay attention to feedback. If discreet mating calls don't win you a positive response, give that person more time and distance. Forget outdated notions about getting "lucky." Make your own luck by using finesse.

FACE READING

Most often, embarrassment is caused by clashing styles with **self-disclosure.** Let me teach you a face reading category that is amazingly helpful for preventing embarrassment.

Whether you're dating or talking with somebody at work, be sure to notice **lipfulness differences** between the two of you.

With very *full lips,* you delight in self-disclosure. So you'll think nothing of divulging juicy details of your life, your emotions, your sex life. To you, it's a way of being authentic. But don't expect other people to share your relish for the juicy stuff. You can easily embarrass a partner with thin lips.

With very *thin lips,* you'll be most comfortable staying with facts, theories, and ideas. Probably you avoid self-disclosure like the plague, and you won't stray from small talk — or business talk or any other kind of on-topic talk — unless you have very good reason.

Beware of blaming other people for embarrassing you just because they're freer with self-disclosure. If they want to tell you things that you would never ask, let them. Then look at those big plump lips and have a secret laugh.

With *moderate lipfulness,* you're unlikely to have problems with embarrassment caused by too much self-disclosure. Instead, judging others is your potential problem. Talking to people whose lips are way fuller or thinner than yours, don't expect them to share your communication style.

After the Honeymoon

Facial opposites can attract powerfully… for the first six months. The one with thin lips is charmed by the one with full lips. Eventually, embarrassment can set in. Don't think your only recourse is collagen injections for the one with the smaller mouth.

+ Should your lover's lavish style with self-disclosure turn annoying, explain that, for you, "Less is more."
+ If you feel judged for communicating in the way that is natural for you, bring that up, too.

Sometimes one short-but-sweet conversation stops the embarrassment. A problem that was mostly subconscious becomes conscious.

After a wee bit of problem solving, voila! Both of you understand that embarrassment has been caused by a difference in your personal styles with self-disclosure. You stop expecting your lover to be "just like me." It's not such a hard conversation to have Just stick out your lips, full or thin, and move them!

AURAS

If any chakra databank on one of you is tiny, while the other partner has a huge one, bingo! You have found a cause of **preventable** embarrassment. For example, the person who blasts out enormous of emotional oomph may make the other one blush.

Once you become aware of the contrast, automatically you move into a position of strength. Should you have the bigger chakra energy, avoid embarrassment by gently reminding yourself not to overwhelm your partner. Should you have the smaller chakra energy, you have three good options:

+ If you're in a love relationship, discuss your differences openly. Explain what you have noticed and gently request that you need special TLC in that particular area of life. Anyone who loves you should be sympathetic. Besides, he/she may already have noticed.

+ In a work relationship, resolve not to take differences personally. Although you may feel tempted to criticize others for not being "normal," your standards are different, that's all.

+ For both your love life and work life, your best choice long-term is to find someone who can help you to heal the cause of the STUFF in your aura. Life as a whole will go better for you, not only this particular relationship.

Unpreventable embarrassment can be related to major gifts that are encoded in a person's aura. That's right, something positive and wonderful can make others cringe.

What if your partner is a creative genius, ultra-empathic, super-intelligent, or an Olympic-caliber clutter-buster? Sounds great in theory, but it still could make others feel slightly inferior, even squirmy. A person's most marvelous gifts don't announce themselves here at Earth School. No matter how clairvoyant you are, you won't find anything like a billboard. Even Mozart's aura didn't carry this kind of obvious sign.

So you must research an aura to discover your partner's major gifts. Do your usual Preparation Process, as described at Page 25, and set an intention to learn about this person.

Then plug-in at the Distinctive Gifts databank at the Soul Chakra. Ask, "What special gifts does he/she have?"

Or follow up on a hunch by asking the same question at the related databank at a different chakra, a physical gift at the Physical Chakra, a spiritual gift at the Spirituality Chakra, etc.

Accept Gifts, Don't Fight Them

Here's an example of a soul-level gift that could cause embarrassment if you didn't know better. About 1 in 1,000 people was born as a **spiritual transformer**; 1 in 100 has a milder version of this gift.

What does this gift mean? Since birth, he/she has been shaking up other people like a human set of maracas. In his/her presence, people are prodded to evolve faster, emotionally and spiritually.

Say that you're researching at the Soul Chakra. You receive information like "He's a spiritual transformer." What's next? Still plugged-in, ask any follow-up questions you like, such as "What does that mean?"

As a result, you might find a fast-moving pattern of energy, especially strong at the third eye. Visually, it could be associated with a lot of violet or with symbols, like exclamation points. Maybe you'll hear information through words or have sensations in your body or feel a strong emotion. Whatever response you receive will educate you about your partner's distinctive gift.

Once you're aware, notice how other people respond when together with your partner and you. Some will welcome the presence of a transformer, others won't notice and, as you'll undoubtedly discover, some people will resist with all their might.

Sure, these "passive resisters" may blame their discomfort on "embarrassment." Spiritual knowledge, from reading auras, can help you become embarassment proof.

16. Evil

How did you ever wind up with that disgusting creep from your past? Evil isn't obvious. Most "bad" people are simply good people with flaws—many of which you can learn to spot from other chapters in this book. Here I'll show you how to tell whether your partner has a major flaw, be it bad character, a personality disorder, or strong potential for wickedness of any kind.

BODY LANGUAGE

Evil is nearly impossible to spot through nonverbal behavior. Knowing this gives you a big advantage over the gullible majority who believe that bad things happen only to other people.

Sweaty palms, shifty eyes—signs of discomfort like these are a good sign for character, relatively speaking. The person dislikes doing wrong. A sociopath won't mind. Therefore, discomfort won't show.

Fortunately, you have two deeper levels to read. In both of them, major problems *will* show.

FACE READING

Arrested development may warn you that something is amiss. When you're reading somebody older than 30, are there signs of aging? Consider it *good* when asymmetries, lines and wrinkles become more pronounced through the decades. Bags and sags, changes to skin texture — society persuades us that this is soooooooooo bad.

Well, I'm here to tell you that it can be good.

Facial aging is natural. Don't confuse it with a person's **soul vitality vibe,** which has nothing to do with chronological age. You can find seniors with the eye gaze and sprightly movement of teenagers, just as you can meet 20-somethings who are, inwardly, pushing 80.

Aside from a youthful soul vibe, other positive factors—like a healthy lifestyle and expansive spiritual life — help to keep a person looking physically youthful. All this couldn't be more different from arrested development. Someone who physically looks way younger than chronological age may be:

+ Psychologically crippled (e.g., Billy the Kid)
+ Involved in a cult or twisted religion (e.g., Timothy McVeigh)
+ Fascinated by the game of deception (e.g., Robert Hanssen)
+ Or terrified by life (e.g., Osama bin Laden).

To find those all-important nuances, you guessed it. Read auras.

AURAS

Auras are the easiest, most reliable way to learn about evil. Even without formal aura reading, you'll occasionally see someone who makes you shudder. Pay attention. (For example, Google on Images for a photo of the Unabomber. Just don't do it right after you've had lunch.)

Most evil people seem normal or, even, charming until you read their auras. Before you commit to any partnership, avoid problems by using my Three Ways to Tell Evil.

Begin with your usual Preparation Process: Pay attention to your inner awareness, then Get Big and set an intention to learn information at a distance, so the learning process itself will not affect you. (For more details, see Page 25.)

First, plug-in at the Ethics databank in the Physical Chakra and ask, "What kind of reality does this person live in?"

A **sociopath** has something majorly wrong. For instance, I remember when I read bin Laden's photo for a media interview. At the Physical Chakra, it felt like entering into a smelly, dark cellar with creepy crawly monsters. Surprising but true, the terrorist was deep-down terrified.

Second, plug-in at the Spiritual Evolution databank at the Spiritual Chakra and ask, "What inspires this person spiritually?"

For some people, the answer is "Me, me, me… and I'm baaaaaaaad."

They're not joking, either.

Other evil people are into zealotry or superiority or "The end justifies the means."

Finally, plug-in at the Altruism databank at the Emotional Chakra and ask, "How does this person show the he/she cares about others?"

Ice-cold hearts are rare. If you find one, you have found the ultimate auric signature of evil.

Whatever you do, never make excuses for problems at any one of these databanks. Consider yourself warned.

17. FACADES

Who wears a facade? Everyone. It's no more optional than skin. Socially people play different roles, and each one requires a facade. Therefore, no matter how great your integrity, you'll seem different at work or a party, a baseball game versus Thanksgiving dinner.

Pity the socially clueless. They look and act the same everywhere.

Still, some facades go on so thick, it's like too much gloppy icing on the cake. How much excess are you and your partner wearing? In this chapter you'll learn how to tell.

BODY LANGUAGE

Hairstyles are the simplest way to read façades. How trendy is your do, especially when compared with your partner's? Is it worn with confidence?

And just how elaborate a coiffure does that partner expect of you anyway? Over the years, those grooming minutes add up. Entire years of your life could be gone with the wind (in your hairdryer).

At work, a partner may not say a thing. Still, your success may be directly proportional to how well you manage "good hair."

Footwear also reveals facades. Compare your partner's everyday shoes with your own. Which of you cares more about current style, sophistication, shine, and big price tag?

Also do both of you move as though the shoes are reasonably comfortable? Does fashion matter more than fit, facade more than kindness to self?

For a love relationship, check out his/her entire wardrobe, if possible. For research, you'll hit the jackpot, a full survey of social facades contained in just one closet.

Makeup standards show facades, too. What do you and your partner expect of each other? Often you can tell by observing others in his/her office or circle of friends. For some groups, **cosmetic surgery** is considered a form of makeup. Decide how you feel about that.

With a lover, educate yourself about facade requirements by meeting the people your partner respects the most. Their facade choices can reflect deep social and spiritual values.

Beware the lover who claims superiority and tries to change you. One sign is being given "presents" that are more-or-less thinly disguised attempts to upgrade your image.

Reading Handshakes QUIZ

Use the five questions below to become an expert handshake analyst. Learn how **down-to-earth** your partner is. Or, if you choose, read **character**. You can even read handshakes to **preview a date sexually**. Check the answers that best match your experience.

1. GRASP: How does the hand-shaker grasp your hand?
   [ ] You must take the lead
   [ ] The hand-shaker takes the lead
   [ ] Cooperatively (Together you ease into the shake.)
   [ ] Too quickly
   [ ] Too slowly (Isn't it time for both of you to get a grip?)
   [ ] Commandingly (Your hand is taken up before you feel
       you have finished offering it.)

2. POSITION: Which part of the hand makes contact with yours?
   [ ] Full palm
   [ ] Palm plus *outer* edge only
   [ ] Palm plus *thumb* edge only
   [ ] Edges of hand, no center
   [ ] Partial palm (excluding the palm near the thumb joint)

3. FEELING DURING: While you shake hands, you feel...
[ ] Comfortable
[ ] Uncomfortable
[ ] Energized
[ ] Drained
[ ] The shake feels too hard
[ ] The shake feels too limp
[ ] Firmness just right

4. RELEASE: How does the handshake end?
[ ] You're dropped like a hot potato
[ ] Sweet! It's like a caress.
[ ] Together you squeeze and let go
[ ] The shake seemed too long
[ ] The shake seemed too quick
[ ] Duration of handshake felt just right

5. FEELING AFTER: And your gut-level feeling right after you let go is?

For answers, turn the page.

FACE READING

Face reading makes it easy to compare your partner's facade in public to the version lived at home. Physically compare the right and left sides of the face. How different are they?

Each physical asymmetry can represent a meaningful difference of façade. Wherever you find a big difference, track down the meaning by using the FACE READING INDEX in the back of this book.

AURAS

Someone who lies repeatedly can lose the ability to distinguish truth from falsehood. By the same token, someone with ultra-thick facades can forget how to live more simply.

Extreme dependence on facades can be read instantly in auras. Begin with your usual Preparation Process: Pay attention to your inner awareness, then Get Big and set an intention to learn the truth about this person. (For more details, see Page 25.)

Plug-in at the Facades databank in the Communication Chakra on the *right* side of the throat and ask, "How hard does he/she work to impress people?"

This will tell you about facades at work.

For facades in personal relationships, plug-in at the Facades databank in the Communication Chakra on the *left* side of the throat and ask, "How hard does he/she work to impress people?"

Bam! You're receiving the scoop about personal life, data galore about quality of facade as well as intensity. You know what you like. It's probably similar to what you'll find in your own databanks.

Reading Handshakes QUIZ ANSWERS

1. GRASP: How does the hand-shaker grasp your hand?

You must take the lead. Do you like taking the lead? In this relationship, you may have to get used to it.

The hand-shaker takes the lead. Hope you like having your partner take the lead, because it's unlikely to stop with the handshake.

Cooperatively. This style augurs well for mutuality in your relationship.

Too quickly. Do you sense over-eagerness? Shyness being overcome? Or maybe this is simply a person whose reaction time is faster than your own, i.e., Not a good ping-pong buddy unless you like to lose… but he/she could inspire you as a friend.

Too slowly Does it take longer than normal for you and the hand-shaker to agree on a grip? Why? Is he/she playing games this early in the relationship? Or could this just be someone with a slower reaction time than yours? (Maybe there could be a ping-pong game in your future after all.)

Commandingly Love it or hate it, but notice it: Your hand-shaker prefers to take charge.

2. POSITION: Which part of the hand makes contact with yours?

Full palm symbolizes full willingness to connect with you.

Palm plus *outer edge only* emphasizes the hand-shaker's aggression.

Palm plus *thumb edge only* suggests a high-maintenance personality, i.e., "It's all about me."

Edges of hand, *no center,* will be especially significant. In terms of auras, palms are sub-chakras about emotion. Contact palm-to-palm symbolizes willingness to connect emotionally. When someone won't, he/she may well have intimacy issues.

Partial palm definitely warns you about lack of emotional depth in relationships.

3. FEELING DURING: While you shake hands, you feel...

Your gut-level emotion when you first touch is enormously important. Puhleeze, don't think there must be an all-important romantic spark or else the two of you have no chemistry. No, what matters is simply your having a reaction that is positive rather than negative.

Comfortable is a good sign.

Uncomfortable isn't necessarily bad. Explore what's going on. Maybe this person reaches deeper into your soul than you're used to.

Energizing. Excellent! You're setting the pattern for the relationship. Thirty years from now, this delightful person could still be a valued partner for work or play.

Draining. Uh-oh. Could the hand-shaker be coercive or needy? Don't put your discomfort into denial. What is your body trying to tell you?

Too hard. What does this person have to prove?

Too limp. Unless your idea of a fun date is dining on over-cooked pasta, you might choose to pass on this as a love relationship.

Firmness just right. For work or play, the two of you could be a good match.

4. RELEASE: How does the handshake end?

You're dropped like a hot potato. Maybe it's lack of sexual sophistication. Or your hand-shaker could be a user. Or both.

You feel caressed. Someone's touch has opened your heart. This could be the start of something great.

Together you squeeze and let go. Right from the start you show mutuality and teamwork, auguring well for your relationship.

Too long. Romantic, seductive or just plain pushy? It's your judgment call, so make it.

Too quick. Shyness could be a factor. Or the hand-shaker could be into quickies. Quality of eye gaze may help you to tell the difference.

Duration of handshake *just right.* Score a point for compatibility.

5. FEELING AFTER: And your gut-level feeling right after you let go is what?

Even if subtle, your *gut-level emotion* about this handshake overall matters more than anything else you have noticed.

Now that you're back to being just you, not physically connecting with this person, how do you feel about yourself?

Every relationship makes you feel a certain way about yourself when you're back to being on your own. Is it good or bad?

Deep down, beneath any facade, you know the truth.

18. Fidelity

The sexual version of loyalty, fidelity does far more than protect your feelings. In the era of AIDS, fidelity has become a matter of life or death. Should you trust the one who's sending you the "Come hither" vibes? Or would it be smart to run thither, top speed?

BODY LANGUAGE

For your lover to hit on somebody else, in your presence, reveals more than infidelity. Dare I use the word "stupidity"?

Still, it happens. You'll know if you see these symptoms of **suggestive behavior:** Prolonged staring, a swaggering walk that emphasizes chest or hips, tossing that too-cute hairstyle or stroking it, touching his/her own body, licking his/her lips in a manner reminiscent of the Big Bad Wolf when Little Red Riding Hood enters the scene.

Although it doesn't seem fair, the behaviors that turned *you* on when directed at *you* will not lose their appeal when directed at *somebody else.* Should you catch your lover at this, the intoxicating brew of seduction may turn to poison.

Just as deadly, for a relationship, is infidelity **behind your back.** By definition, this body language is hard to read. Yet you don't want to be blind to the possibility.

One safeguard is to screen a date for infidelity in the early stages of your relationship. Initiate a "getting to know you and your values" conversation and, as part of it, pop this question: "How important is fidelity to you?"

When the answer comes, let your ears read between the lines. Does the **tone of voice** become unusually sarcastic, bitter, angry, or heavily charged with any emotion? Not a good sign.

Look next for **protective gestures,** such as crossed arms or posture that becomes visibly uptight.

Notice postural **mixed messages,** such as a partner who faces you but avoids your eyes, or vice versa. Also, pay attention if he/she faces toward you but keeps shoulders tilted away.

Finally, be aware that during a conversation like this, **flirtatious gestures,** like pouting, can mean that your lover uses sex as a means to play games about power, attractiveness, money or trust.

In a long-term relationship, temptation can afflict even committed partners who value fidelity. So don't stop your research with body language. Clues are much easier to read at deeper levels.

FACE READING

Hopefully, your partner's face will reveal signs of LOYALTY. (See Page 163.) For infidelity, don't expect to spot anything as clear-cut as The Scarlet Letter in Nathaniel Hawthorne's novel. In real life, you're better off making a study of chins.

A **dimpled chin** reveals temptation to question commitments, especially if the chin is also long.

This could play out as a series of monogamous relationships... or worse. But this face data also marks someone who takes a creative approach to life in general. Not so bad!

A **Macho Knob** looks like a doorknob—a circular wad of muscle, sometimes very raised and fleshy.

The owner of such a chin may be tempted to be unfaithful due to wounded pride.

The positive side of this trait is strong appreciation for maleness. If a man has the Knob, masculinity is an important value. To stay faithful, he needs to have that manly ego stroked on a regular basis.

A woman with the Knob values a "strong man" and needs for him to act in ways that make her feel proud to be with him.

AURAS

If everybody knew about **the three-day problem,** fidelity might become more common.

Whenever you're sexually intimate, your lover's aura blends with yours for three days.

That's right, count three cycles of 24 hours. Deeper than any tell-tale lipstick smudge, infidelity is aurically obvious. Your energy fields will mingle long after the afterplay, with special emphasis at your second chakra.

Sexual intercourse will produce this result, and so will a good make-out session.

Therefore, infidelity complicates your aura as well as your sex life. Say that the same day you, Lover A, hop into the sack with Lover B... somewhere else your spouse, Lover C, chooses to dally with Lover D. Both you and your spouse will soon have a whole lot in common: Auras with A + B + C + D.

Thus, if you're dating someone who's married, aurically you're making it with that spouse. Consider yourself a threesome. Unless there's more he/she isn't telling you.

So, if you want to make sure that your lover stays true to you, read his/her aura every few days. Any databank will do.

Get used to that auric presence. Then you can tell instantly if someone else is sharing the bod.

19. Flirtatiousness

When someone flirts with you, is it special treatment or merely standard operating procedure? Players are experts at flirting. To keep yourself from being hurt by one — or just for fun —educate yourself about the teasing, pleasing art of playing at love.

BODY LANGUAGE

Flirtation starts with a **rhythm.** Someone who flirts with you pays attention, then hides. Or moves closer, then backs away.

Switching the love light on, he/she will prolong eye contact, offer a special smile, give expansive gestures that welcome you with open arms.

Other **signs of flirtation** include crossing or uncrossing legs, subtle movements of the hands or feet, and a head that cocks to one side.

More intimate components of flirtation include a seductive tone of voice, uplifted eyebrows when gazing in your direction. Pouting lips are, of course, popular.

Overall, a big flirt will turn up your overall level of **sexual self-consciousness.** Sense it rising off your lover's body like steam off a radiator?

Flirtatiousness is more contagious than a yawn. So don't dismiss it as your personal quirk if you flash back to an earlier time in your life when you felt your first sexual awakening.

Yes, flirtatiousness is an easy kind of body language to respond to. And read. But the body language you share as a couple gives no clue about whether this is a big romance or just a big romancer. For research that could make all the difference for your future happiness, investigate the deeper levels of face reading and aura reading.

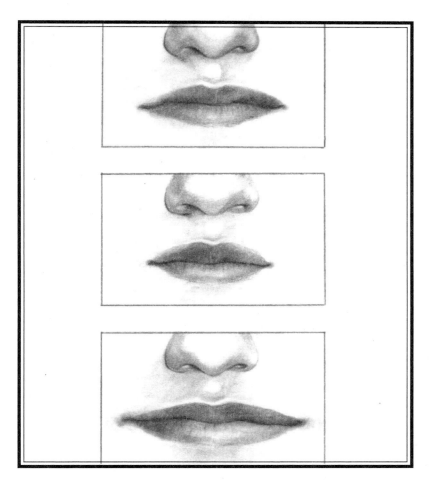

Illustration 13. LIP LENGTH

Medium, short or long? To gauge mouth length, you won't always have a set of three matched illustrations, the way we do here.

Usually, you will use the person's overall facial proportions as your guide, including nose length, nose tip width, jaws and chin.

If I didn't have this matched set for comparison, I wouldn't try to read the mouth lengths here — not enough data.

25 Signs of Attraction

"They're playing our song," even if nobody else in the room can hear music. Ah! When this happens to you and your lover, you're definitely attracted.

But romance is one thing. Lust is another. Make sure you're reading the signals right. Moving in too fast can make you seem crude. Find at least four signs of attraction before you pucker up.

1. Facial expression, on the whole, is exceptionally animated.
2. Eyes blink more than usual, accompanied by flirtatious glances.
3. Or the pupils dilate.
4. Or eyes become brighter, shinier.
5. Or eyes hold your gaze for a fraction longer than necessary.
6. Oops, you catch your lover staring at you, and then he/she looks away, embarrassed.
7. Self-consciousness shows in lips, such as a slight pouting or quivering.
8. Or the lips are moistened.
9. Or licked.
10. Or lips part (without words are being spoken).
11. Or lips might be drawn inward, shyly.
12. Or they pout.
13. A hand flies up to cover the lips, then moves down.
14. Not just eyes but the whole face turns toward you, then moves away.
15. Nostrils flare.
16. Breathing pattern changes (although there has been no change in physical activity).
17. The head tilts to one side, with the chin closer to you than the forehead.

18. *Hair is patted or stroked.*
19. *Or he/she plays with a ring of hair.*
20. *Fingers stroke part of the face.*
21. *The torso tilts toward you. (And, for a man, the 3-D effect may be especially obvious.)*
22. *A hand moves, angling toward you.*
23. *A foot moves, angling toward you.*
24. *Fidgeting begins (when fidgets are not typical behavior for this person).*
25. *Fingers move self-consciously, as in "Gawsh, what am I supposed to do with my hands if I have to keep them off* **you?**"

FACE READING

Lip length is your single best way to gauge flirtatiousness through the face.

+ The *longer* the lips, the more often a natural friendliness is extended to everyone.
+ With a *short* mouth, seduction comes through sincerity—the enticement of an intense one-on-one conversation.
+ Finally, *moderate* mouth length indicates flexible flirtatiousness: sometimes crowd-pleasing, sometimes highly personal.

To learn more about flirtatious tendencies on a person with long lips, also read **lipfulness.**

Should the long lips also be *full,* the flirtatious impulse is stronger, with a more personal content to the conversation.

By contrast, with *thin* lips, flirting takes on a more intellectual character. A dry, ironic wit will be on display. And the subtext may be "Stroke my ego but if you touch me physically, I'll be shocked! Shocked!"

AURAS

As possible love problems go, a tendency toward flirtatiousness need not be a deal breaker. You might even admire a lover's ability to string others along when, as both of you know, you're still the main squeeze.

Both of you could even be outrageous flirts who can meet-up at the end of the day and laugh over your conquests.

It isn't unheard of to have a lifestyle where everybody swings and everybody's happy.

Nobody else can decide for you what you prefer sexually. Just know what you're signing on for before the ship leaves the dock.

To research flirtatiousness aurically, start with your usual Preparation Process: Pay attention to your inner awareness, then Get Big and set an intention to enjoy this exploration into your partner. (For more details, see Page 25.)

Plug-in at the Sexual Chakra, move into the Flirtation databank and ask, "How does he/she feel about flirting?"

Just as some folks are compulsive liars, some are compulsive flirts. If your lover 's aura shows huge energy here, you might want to supplement your research with an extra databank about authenticity:

Plug-in at the *left* side of his/her Communication Chakra, researching the databank about Integrity in Intimate Relationships.

Ask, "How genuine is his/her flirtation with me?" Notice if there's an oily, seductive or otherwise tricky component to this part of the aura.

But you also might find the energetic equivalent of bells, whistles, roses, balloon bouquets. You may be wildly delighted. More power to you both!

20. Guilt

Darn, has somebody caught you feeling guilty again? Relax. *Feeling* guilty doesn't necessarily equate with *being* guilty.

You'll know the difference about yourself. But how can you tell with your partner? Deeper perception can help you to sort out variations on the theme of guilt.

The truly nasty, naughty stuff shows in body language and auras, while self-doubt masquerading as guilt is best discerned through face reading.

BODY LANGUAGE

When someone who usually meets your eyes suddenly won't, the reason could be guilt. Other warning signs include slumped-over posture, fidgets and big neon letters with a pointing arrow (just joking about that last one).

Vocal clues are a strained tone of voice, volume that trails off mid-sentence, or super-hearty over-confidence.

But the strongest danger sign is a **change** to your partner's usual patterns of body language. Once this alerts you that something may be wrong, go straight to the aura for more conclusive detective work. If the problem's not guilt, what is it?

FACE READING

Could someone feel destined for a life of remorse, despite being innocent of any wrongdoing?

Four facial characteristics relate to guiltless guilt. They are what I call **soul signature traits.** Unlike 9 out of 10 bits of face data, which can change over time, certain aspects of a face stay around for keeps. These soul signature traits are related to a person's life contract and are not likely to change over time. Four of these soul signature traits are related to inner patterns of feeling guilt.

Cleft chins signal remorse over major life choices. Even when your partner has done nothing wrong, he/she may fear having made big mistakes.

Petite chins, small in proportion with the rest of the face, go with ultra-high ethical standards. The corresponding challenge is feeling guilty over the tiniest shortcomings. (Ironically, it's the folks with extra-large chins who are more likely to do something for which guilt feelings would be appropriate.)

Crossed front teeth overlap at the edges. Even though subtle, this tooth trait is worth noticing. It alerts you to confidence issues. Remember, self-imposed guilt doesn't necessarily correlate with wrongdoing. Have compassion! This person's life contract involves major lessons in self-confidence.

Crooked bottom teeth suggest that a person will sometimes wrestle with temptation. Dealing with the consequences, guilt might or might not be an appropriate reaction. But typically nobody suffers as much as the worrier.

So whether the one with the built-in guilt data is you or your partner, be kind. All of us are tested in life. Wrestling with one's conscience tests character. If anything, the chin and tooth characteristics described here mean that the person is good, not bad.

AURAS

Guilt in an aura is bad news… but also good news, in a weird way. Sociopaths don't suffer from guilt, so if you can feel it, congratulations! Guilt can motivate personal growth.

Luckily, the guilt that shows in auras comes complete with nuances. To find them, start with your usual Preparation Process: Pay attention to your inner awareness, then Get Big and set an intention to explore confidently. (For more details, see Page 25.)

To find out if you can trust your lover, plug-in at the Conscience databank in the Emotional Chakra and ask, "What's going on now emotionally?"

If you find guilt, follow up by silently asking if this pattern is recent or chronic.

A second place to seek guilt is at the Physical Chakra. Plug-into the Personal Responsibility databank and ask, "Are you satisfied right now with how you have lived your life?" Trauma can be accompanied by guilt feelings until the trauma is healed. Eventually the "culprit" learns to distinguish between guilt, taking unnecessary responsibility for other people's problems, being human, etc.

Don't expect an aura to come complete with subtitles, e.g., "This blob of guilt comes from cheating on my ex with our next-door neighbor, Taylor." You can find polite ways to steer conversation toward the topic of guilt—or auras—and discuss what has been happening.

Sometimes life hands us dilemmas with no easy solution. If that happens to you or your partner, maybe it's time to push the boundaries of the relationship. Guilt that results from tough choices can be lightened by sharing. If your partner is also a friend, you'll be able to tell your whole story, including the tough parts.

Someone who can hear about your deepest pain without flinching, someone who remembers to be kind when you are vulnerable, that good friend is a keeper.

Beware "The Naughty Affirmation"

One trick of language can make all the difference between feeling good about yourself vs. feeling guilty. Don't use "The Naughty Affirmation."

This is a common phrase that accumulates in the subconscious mind with crippling force. Be on the lookout, the listen-out, for these very dangerous words: "I don't know."

If your partner says this during a conversation, don't stand for it. Insist that he/she stop being evasive or lazy or hopeless or careless or drunk or passively waiting for someone else to make all the choices.

And if it's you, follow the Buddha's example. He planted himself beneath the Bodhi tree, refusing to get up until he became enlightened. You're not demanding mega-enlightenment here, merely self-honesty. Probably you won't have to skip more than eight or nine meals!

It's true. You and your partner, both, have a preference regarding *any* question that involves a feeling, an opinion, or a choice.

+ Could you be scared to admit it?
+ Could you be used to lying to yourself?
+ Could you be avoiding information that contrasts with what you prefer to believe, even if that isn't true?

Any of these patterns can lead to guilt. Let yourself consciously know what, deep down, you do know.

Then you can decide yes or no. Call it self-honesty or simply self-acceptance. Either way, it's the opposite of feeling guilty.

You set your own curriculum here at Earth School. Your feelings, thoughts and wishes are all part of it. So what's the worst that can happen if you admit the truth to yourself?

Personally, I'm a big believer in positive thinking. Yet I've seen people use positivity to numb themselves into "I don't know."

Failure follows. Then the well meaning seeker has one yet more reason to feel guilty.

Recognize how you feel. Then you have an authentic person using those good affirmations.

After making contact with yourself, you'll have more success using any positive beliefs, plus any self-improvement method of your choice. Don't play with "The Secret" as a diversion from keeping secrets (like guilt) from yourself.

21. Hurt Feelings

Even in fairy tales, the "happily ever after" part doesn't happen until the end. In real life, emotional pain can be scripted into any part of your story, from start to end. Even if both partners have the kindest intentions, pain is a risk.

What if one of you happens to be emotionally accident prone, with a tendency either to hurt your partner's feelings or to have them hurt? Protect yourself by reading deeper.

BODY LANGUAGE

Not everyone knows how to read hurt feelings through body language, yet it's easy to do.

After hurt has escalated, it will show in a **long-held expression,** but you're better off cuing in earlier, when pain first starts. For this, read the signs in **micro-expressions.** (See Page 9.) Either slow or fast, chronic or fleeting, here are the first signs of hurt feelings:

Eyes express pain with clenching of the lower eyelids or simply an inward focus.

If you're extra-perceptive, you may also discern a shift in **eye glitter,** how soul light beams through the eyes. Every significant mood expresses through eye glitter, including hurt.

Lips are equally revealing. Lips say "hurt" by moving into a distorted position, a contrast to how those lips are usually held, such as either drawing lips closer together to keep the pain from showing or "bravely" stretching the lips extra-wide to create a facade of indifference.

If you choose to specialize in reading hurt from facial expression, you'll learn how to find it in cheeks, jaws, chins, eyebrows, and foreheads. In innumerable, ingenious ways, people try (and fail) to keep their pain from showing.

Showing the Hurt

Our body language survey of hurt feelings wouldn't be complete without discussing exaggeration.

Pouting is the most common method, where the lower lip sticks out in loud nonverbal protest. But why settle for unadorned pouting? It's so much more interesting when other facial muscles get into the act.

Whenever long-held expressions are used intentionally for purposes of display, the effect can be dramatic. For instance, have you ever wondered where women learn how to perfect "the hurt look"? That's the one which says, "You're in big trouble now."

Mom taught it. And some sons learn it just fine, too. Sons who become players, or hold lots of STUFF, are especially likely to use this expression.

Hurt can also be expressed nonverbally through **sounds** like sighs, groans and grunts. Some partners make these sounds purposely to hint that feelings have been hurt.

It's unfair to hint, and even worse to demand ultra-high maintenance, as in "If you really loved me, you'd have noticed."

Don't play by such rules yourself. When you're hurt, don't hint. Communicate directly, especially when it's not a work relationship.

What can you do when a friend blames you for hurt feelings? Discuss it. Assuming that you explore, rather than accuse, the resulting conversation may strengthen your relationship.

In fact, it might be useful for both of you to discuss how each of you signals hurt feelings. (Tactfully, call it "being upset." And have this conversation at a time when you're both getting along.)

Figure it out, one way or another. Otherwise hurt feelings will leak out behaviorally, maybe escalating over time. You could even agree on some funny nonverbal signals, like pulling an earlobe to mean "Oh, I'm just sobbing now. Get down on your knees right away and beg for forgiveness." The job description for friendship should *not* include reading minds.

FACE READING

A partner may hurt your feelings unintentionally because the two of you have such different personal styles about some aspect of life. Face reading is unsurpassed for quickly revealing these differences. For instance, see our chapters about CONFORMITY, SELF-DIS-CLOSURE, and SENSITIVITY.

In this chapter, I want to show you how to avoid hurt feelings by reading the shape at the **bottom edge** of the lower lip.

+ Usually it's *curved,* more or less. Curve symbolizes communicating in a way that takes other people's feelings into account.

+ By contrast, a *straight lower lip* suggests blunt speech—effective in the workplace but not necessarily considerate.

If you're the one with the straight-lipped style, do what you can to honor your partner's feelings when discussing controversial topics.

+ Harder to control is a *blade-like lower lip,* which combines three physical characteristics. It's wider in the center than at the edges; the mouth, in general, is long; and the lower lip also tilts inwards.

(Oops, when George Bush Sr. said, "Read my lips," he offered physiognomists a perfect speciment of a blade-like lower lip. I hasten to add that his face counters this with plenty of loveable attributes. Just ask his wife, Barbara.)

It's unlikely that you'll ever find a baby born with a blade-like mouth. It's shaped over years of ruthless self-interest, resulting in unthinking cruelty.

Although this represents a danger to your feelings, someone with a mouth like this may use that no-nonsense communication style to be spectacularly successful.

Just draw the line at unkind treatment in your relationship. Only martyrs go quietly!

AURAS

Which people attract your interest? They can have emotional problems that match yours like pieces of a jigsaw puzzle. One common pairing is **hurter + victim.**

If you have tired of this game, learn to identify both emotional abusers and super-vulnerable victims-in-waiting.

Begin with your usual Preparation Process. Pay attention to your inner awareness, then Get Big and set an intention to be of service to this person. (For more details, see Page 25.)

Plug-in to the Emotional Memories databank at your partner's Emotional Chakra.

+ Does he/she chronically holds hurt.?
+ A strong need to hurt others' feelings will show at this chakra as well.

To find out, ask this question: "How does this person handle emotional pain?"

You'd also be wise to check out the Everyday Power databank at the Power Chakra.

+ If you're reading a date or lover, plug-in at the left side of the solar plexus area and ask, "How does this person deal with power in love relationships?"
+ If you're reading someone at work, plug-in at the right side of the solar plexus area and ask, "How does this person deal with power in work relationships?"

Either way, if you find a strong need to put others down, or become a victim, consider yourself warned.

What if *your* aura is the one to show problems with hurt? You don't have to be full-blown sadist or masochist to deserve some help. Find a psychotherapist, pastoral counselor, regression therapist, or energy healer. Better the temporary hurt to your pride, admitting there's a problem, than a lifetime of suffering.

22. Intelligence

Let's face it. Intelligence comes second only to sexiness in the Falling for Fantasies Department. Such vast differences between what is assumed, pretended, and wished for! Let deeper perception save you from duh's about smarts.

BODY LANGUAGE

During the courtship phase, you and your partner are likely to experiment with more varied activities and conversations than at any other time in your relationship. Use these opportunities to assess intelligence.

What do different conversational topics do for **engagement?** Posture will become more alert when a subject really matters. What kind of conversation lights up those eyes?

Use what you learn to fill in the chart about **Intellectual Compatibility** on the following page.

Next, research how your partner uses hand motions to communicate. **Ideographic gestures** go with the overall pattern of the words being spoken, e.g., As a story builds to its climax, the movements become bigger and more expressive. This kind of gesture shows that your partner has a flair for abstract thought.

By contrast, **physiographic gestures** are the conversational equivalent of show-and-tell, like a lip-synch performance.

For "It was a huge pizza," arms wave wide, progressing to "And I ate the whole thing," where the stomach is clutched and the face assumes the blank look of the Pillsbury Doughboy.

Physiographic gestures reveal physical intelligence, maybe also sensuality... with love of pizza being optional.

Intellectual Compatibility

We're all smart. Right! We're sure not all smart in the same way. Based on what you have observed so far, fill out this chart. Assess what you have now, then what you find in the partner you have in real life. Also complete your wish list for the partner of your dreams, the one you'd have if you never, ever had to settle.

Cross out any uninteresting categories and write in ones you prefer. Do you like when a lover can carry a tune? Add up restaurant tabs without a calculator? It's smart to know what you like.

TYPE OF INTELLIGENCE	MY TALENTS	MY PARTNER NOW	MY IDEAL PARTNER
Social			
Verbal			
Mathematical			
Mechanical			
Musical			
Spatial			
Athletic			
Nature-Loving			
Spiritual			
Political			

FACE READING

Investigate intelligence further by reading **eye glitter**, how soul light reflects from your partner's eyes. (Note: You're better off learning to read this in person, rather than from pictures, where photographer's lighting can mask natural eye glitter.)

Quiet yourself inside. Gaze into your partner's eyes. Then ask inwardly, "Which kind of intelligence is uppermost?" Answers come as intuition. Don't expect a literal answer, like tiny print stretched across each eyeball.

You can ask about each of the categories on the opposite page and receive information accordingly.

To discern more nuances, read the **brightness** of eyes. (Want to develop your eye for these subtleties? You'll have to read many people, not just your partner.)

+ The *brighter* the eyes, the greater the amount of intelligence.
+ Some eyes specialize in a *penetrating* light, which means perceptiveness.
+ *Steady*, strong glitter conveys exceptional power at focusing the mind.
+ With *moderate* brightness, the person is smart but not brilliant.
+ *Dull* light — lights on but maybe nobody home — can indicate a problem with substance abuse. So can *erratic* or *scary* light coming from eyes.

AURAS

You can learn even more about intelligence by going directly to the ultimate encyclopedia of talent, the human energy field.

Begin with your usual Preparation Process: Pay attention to your inner awareness, then Get Big and set an intention to gain wisdom. (For more details, see Page 25.)

Plug-in at the Intelligence databank in the Power Chakra. Ask, "What is happening now with this person's intelligence?"

Not only can you receive detailed, nuanced particulars. You can also research blockages, like lack of self-confidence.

That, of course, can be healed over time. In my highly cerebral terminology, it's only STUFF.

Don't forget to ask this follow-up question: "Intellectually, what are his/her strongest gifts of the soul?"

At work, use what you find to strengthen relationships. Talk in terms of your partner's keenest intelligence. Your partner will shine... and love you for it.

Dale Carnegie has helped millions to succeed in business with his bestselling book, *How to Win Friends and Influence People*. His secrets of success still work today, but they work far better if you supplement them with deeper perception.

Who is that person, really? What kind of intelligence predominates? Speak to that and your strategically placed words will have maximum impact.

Reading intelligence can also help you succeed at love relationships. Often people talk about fanning the flame of love. Well, why not fan the flame of intelligence while you're at it?

Find out what interests your lover. Then seek ways to make discussion part of your regular routine.

With intelligence specialties in mind, ask questions about what he/she has been learning lately.

Explore new interests together, take trips, or buy books related to mutual kinds of curiosity. (See more about this on Page 176.)

Imagine being in a relationship where you talk deep into the night and wake up curious to learn even more. You can have that.

23. INTIMACY

How close is too close? Two perfectly sane people may have wildly different answers. (And since when have two people in love been perfectly sane, anyway?)

The good news is, any pairing of intimacy styles can be compatible. That goes for work as well as play.

Intimacy extremes, like smothering and neglect, wreck relationships. And once intimacy inflammation sets in… it can be harder to cure than herpes. So learn these fascinating ways to read personal boundaries.

BODY LANGUAGE

Proxemics, the study of distance in body language, is your first clue to intimacy boundaries. Each of us has habits about keeping a certain physical distance from others.

We may adjust borders differently for strangers, friends and partners. Still these social boundaries form a pattern, shaped partly by individual temperament, partly by cultural background.

When you visit with your family, does everybody stand close? Then don't expect instant comfort with a partner whose family does just the opposite. Have fun noticing proxemics at family gatherings.

Meanwhile, you can compare distance styles between just the two of you. What if you and your partner have drastically different habits about distance with physical space?

Don't take it personally. The simplest solution may be adjusting to your partner's comfort zone.

If that makes you uncomfortable, though, it's time to talk. Educate your partner about proxemics, then play with the possibilities. Together you two can figure out how to get close… not too close, just close enough.

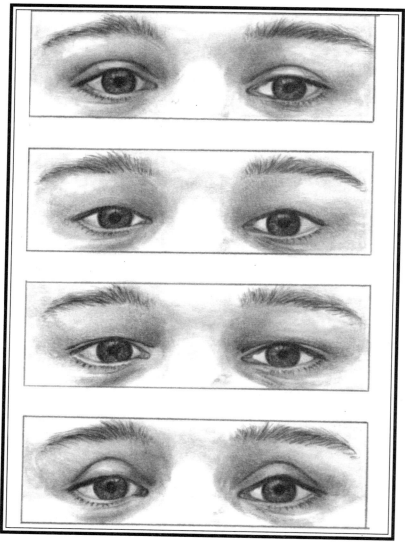

Illustration 14. EYELIDS

Find single and double eyelids. Then, among those double eyelids, can you spot the amounts of eyelid thickness that I call *full*, *even*, and *none?* See any *cut-offs?* For answers, turn the page.

FACE READING

Which matters more for your peace of mind, feeling close to others or having plenty of personal space? How about your partner? Read eyelids to find out.

Start by exploring **eyelid fold,** which reveals deep expectations about personal space. Most people in the West have double eyelids, where the skin folds once beneath the brow bone, framing the eye socket. By contrast, single eyelids lack that fold but, instead, drop straight down from brow bone to eyelashes. (Use depth perception, to help you see eyelid fold clearly.)

+ With *double eyelids,* deep down you relate to life as an individualist. You come first. Other people come second.

+ By contrast, with *single eyelids,* you feel connected to your family and to society in general. (Whether this gives you incentive to act extra-considerate or merely makes you feel guilty, eyelids alone won't show.)

Next, let's can add the highly individual factor of **eyelid thickness.** This means the size of the fold that shows from the front.

To see this, it may help to imagine that the person you're reading has put on the cosmetic called "eyeshadow." Weird or not, fantasize that your partner's lids have been enhanced with shimmering blue powder. How much of that makeup would show when his/her eyes are open?

+ A lot of eyelid counts as *full* eyelid thickness, sometimes called "bedroom eyes."

+ A smallish, but even, amount, officially counts as *even.*

+ *None* is also possible. Usually you'll find this with a single eyelid, but it's also quite common with double eyelids as well. For practical purposes, a tiny amount, or partially *cut-off* eyelid thickness also counts as "none."

+ Single eyelids do sometimes have an extra rim of eyelid fold. I call this *the double whammy.*

What can eyelids reveal about intimacy style? If your partner's needs are exactly the opposite of yours, the two of you may need to practice seeing life through each other's eyelids.

+ Full eyelids correspond to the need to be very close, while the reverse signals emotional independence.
+ With no eyelid thickness, or with cut-offs, your partner needs plenty of personal space.
+ With the double whammy, your partner strives to be considerate, then tries extra-hard to get even closer.
+ Finally, even eyelids mean "no issues around intimacy," but there still could be STUFF, so check out that aura.

AURAS

Intimacy blockage big enough to cause trouble will show in an aura.

Armoring is the technical term for long-term blockage that keeps out intimacy. Self-protectiveness can cause a guy or gal to put a wall up, emotionally. Yes, you may have found walls on yourself or your partner already, when researching auras in our chapters on CONFIDENCE, EMBARRASSMENT, FACADES, HURT FEELINGS, and more.

Sometimes people try to "tighten boundaries" or "put up walls" or "construct shields" because they don't know any bet-

---

Illustration 14. QUIZ ANSWERS

Taking our set of four drawings from the top:
+ *Double* eyelid fold, also *even* eyelid thickness.
+ *Single* eyelid fold. Eyelid thickness here counts as *none.*
+ *None.* (Both these eyelids show some *cut-off* in the center. Can you tell which one has more? Give yourself extra credit if you see that the right eye has more cut-off than the left.)
+ *Full* eyelid thickness.

ter. Sound familiar? Probably you believe that you're protecting yourself. Reconsider. Unwittingly, you could be pushing your real friends away.

Unskilled empaths often put up walls just to cope with their special sensitivity. Actually, skilled empaths never need walls. Instead, thay learn special ways to use their consciousness.

With training, you can wake up inside until you become the most important person in the room wherever you go. That vibrant presence protects you far better than any wall.

Sexual reserve is another reason why some people misguidedly put up walls. Huge sexual charisma, or simply having a very hot body, can bring unwanted attention.

Walls aren't a good solution, though. They don't protect auras. Unskilled empaths, putting up walls, still pick up other people's fear and pain. Ironically, it stays stuck in an aura *inside* that wall. Sexually, walls will keep their owner from fully enjoying sex with *anyone.*

Why? How much intimacy would you have if you wore a suit of armor? That's what walls are like, only they usually surround just one chakra, not your entire body.

You can have walls around your Physical Chakra, your Spiritual Chakra, any chakra. Unlike a metal suit of armor, those walls can't be put on or removed at will. Long as you have them, they're with you 24/7.

But walls in auras are only a form of STUFF. They can always be healed. When they're gone, results will show aurically as well as behaviorally.

If you or your partner have intimacy problems, it's particularly important to avoid becoming sexually involved. Otherwise you may *never* establish a close emotional bond.

Whose choice is wall removal? You guessed it. Love alone doesn't remove longstanding intimacy issues. That isn't a fair test of your partner's love — or your worth.

24. Jealousy

The green-eyed monster lives, so learn to spot this relationship wrecker.

BODY LANGUAGE

Does your partner literally put you on a leash? Well, don't expect jealousy patterns to be that obvious.

On the level of body language, your best bet is to swap life stories and, when it comes to the juicy parts, supplement what you hear by reading **engagement**. (No, silly, I don't mean a diamond ring taken from a box. "Engagement" is a term psychologists use to mean whether or not there's a big emotional charge to the conversation.)

Nonverbal cues to engagement include:

+ *Tone of voice* : A big emotional charge adds intensity to the words.
+ Voice *volume:* Ooh, somebody turned the sound up. Why?
+ *Pronunciation:* Keen listeners can hear subtle changes in how words are spoken. Lack of engagement can bring extra distinctness and duration to consonants like t, p, b and k.
+ *Posture* stiffens: Face and back can become more rigid with intense engagement.
+ *Eyes brighten* or flash: Like the picture on a TV screen, the amount of energy pouring through eyes can turn up or down. With engagement, eyes become more animated.

Sure, engagement can have causes that don't involve jealousy. But danger shows if engagement rises while your date describes the infidelity of a past partner.

Also consider yourself warned if (regardless of body language) your partner expresses suspicion about your fidelity, or demands that you drop all your other friends. That's too high a price to pay for any relationship.

FACE READING

For more secrets related to jealousy, read **cheek padding**. Physically, this facial category means the amount of extra flesh on either side of the face between cheekbone and jaw. It's the stuff an over-affectionate grandma could pinch.

Quick clarification for those of you who share in society's fatness obsession... Does cheek padding equal fat? No way! Skinny people can have full cheeks, while some of their chubbier cousins show an absence of cheek padding.

What's the padding about then, if not weight? For 5,000 years, physiognomists have equated it with social support. Relationship problems can arise at either extreme although, in my system of Face Reading Secrets, each attribute corresponds to a strength, too.

With *big* cheek padding, you easily garner support for your projects. Friends and co-workers are relatively eager to help. (Why just "relatively"? Amount of support depends on who these people are otherwise. You can't squeeze blood from a stone, even if you're a blood drive superstar.)

What's your challenge? It's spending way too much time giving support to others. Earning your reputation as a good sport can feel like the Tooth Gnashing Olympics. There you are, trotting along to the umpteenth boooooooring event that fascinates your buddies.

Jealousy can enter this picture while you're being obliging, as in, "How come they never do this kind of thing for me?"

With *small* cheek padding, your social talent is self-reliance. You've learned to do-it-yourself more often than not, which has strengthened you.

Nonetheless, you have a potential challenge, too: feeling unsupported by others. Your version of jealousy sounds like, "Where's my help when I need it? How come he/she's always *getting* help but never *giving* it?"

With *moderate* cheek padding, you naturally balance giving and receiving social support, so you're unlikely to have suffered from challenges about it… unless you've developed **jowls**.

Wads of hanging flesh, ooching over the sides of a face, can happen to people with any amount of cheek padding. Incidentally, jowls aren't about aging. (If they were, *all* seniors would have them, right?)

No, jowls mean decreased support from former friends and business associates. One can consider it a spiritual invitation to find more strength from within. Still jowls can produce jealousy toward people who *do* still get massive social support.

AURAS

Who feels jealous? To find out, start with your usual Preparation Process: Pay attention to your inner awareness, then Get Big and set an intention to learn the truth. (For more details, see Page 25.)

Read the Unspoken Words databank at the Communication Chakra. Plug-in and ask, "Are there any long-term obstacles to communication?"

For a love relationship, also research the Intimacy databank at the Sexual Chakra. Plug-in and ask, "Are there any long-term obstacles to sexual intimacy?" What you find may open your heart to a new level of compassion, healing tendencies that you may have toward jealousy.

Another possibility is that your research at these chakras will reveal jealousy in your partner.

In that case, know that jealousy strong enough to show in an aura is highly toxic. This disease can't be cured by anyone except the patient. So it may be important to protect yourself by letting the jealous one go.

What if *you* are the one who feels jealous? This pattern is an energy stealer. Seek the healing you need. By the time you're done, you'll believe in yourself.

25. Listening Ability

Which will matter more to you in the long run, having a partner who's good *looking* or good at *listening*? Do investigate, because good listening can be an act, like the sizing put into cheap clothes. After a wash or two, your limp garment bears little resemblance to the crisp shirt that first caught your eye.

BODY LANGUAGE

While you talk about something that matters to you, what happens to your partner's **attentiveness**? Do eyes glaze over or point toward the distance? Not a good sign.

What else shows a good listener? Interested, interesting questions, delivered in a **caring tone of voice,** are harder to fake than goo-goo eyes.

Listening ability also shows in a partner's nonverbal **song and dance.** A listener's love song sounds like plenty of "Uh-huh"s and "Mmm"s, especially powerful when synchronized with the dance of up-and-down head nods. Weigh all this against the percentage of conversation hogged by your partner. Do you get a chance to talk?

FACE READING

First physiognomy cues about listening come from **ear curve.** Follow the outer edge of the left ear. What is the shape?

Most people have *curved ear edges.* The rounder the shape, the more a person unconsciously listens from the heart.

By contrast, someone with *rectangular ear edges* listens more selectively. He/she is like a magnet for information in areas of interest. Anything that might conflict with existing beliefs and interests may be ignored.

Occasionally, you'll meet someone with an *angular ear top*. No, it isn't the sign of an elf (unless the rest of the body is very short and made of shimmering light). In human terms, ears like this correspond to an unusually high degree of unconscious control when listening. This could translate as artistic creativity, dogmatic beliefs or a strong desire to dominate in relationships.

Ear length can also help you to appreciate a person's strengths as a listener. *Long ears* correspond to consistently strong interest in listening to others.

Short ears suggest that your partner listens intently for a while, then overloads. When nonverbal cues show that his/her attentiveness has stopped, make a note to bring the point up later. This strategy works well if your partner's ear length is *moderate,* too. (You just won't need to use it as often.)

AURAS

Don't wait until you're in desperate need to be heard. Find out now if your partner can do it. Research **the blend of heart and mind**.

Begin with your usual Preparation Process: Pay attention to your inner awareness, then Get Big and set an intention to open up to knowledge about your partner. (For more details, see Page 25.)

Now, read the Trusting Emotions databank at the Emotional Chakra. Plug-in and ask, "How does he/she use emotional insight?"

Note the *amount* of emotional energy and the degree of sensitivity. Then explore *quality*. Will you find the super-open heart of an empath, the armoring of a hard-to-reach heart or stored-up STUFF from the past, like resentment? Maybe all three?

Practice on people you know well. Compare what you know about their listening ability with patterns at their emotional chakras. I promise, you'll be so impressed, you'll get hooked on aura reading for life. Who would have guessed the extent to which listening happens with the heart rather than the ears?

Now plug-in at the Trusting Ideas databank at the Power Chakra. Ask, "How does this person balance heart and mind?"

Some minds and hearts work together, others don't. Sure the balance can change, if the person is willing. But someone who lives in the mind, with no heart, isn't likely to change... or to be much of a listener, no matter how much you need it.

Does Your Partner Think the World of You?

Nonverbally, you have your own world. Body language experts call it your **kinesphere,** *the horizontal and vertical space in which a person moves. Think of it as a bubble created by your posture and gestures.*

Although there's no such thing as a "bad kinesphere," sometimes relationships get stuck because the two partners have—Dare I say it?— **incompatible kinespheres.**

A partner who thinks the world of you does not grudge the space you take up. Conversely, if you're often told, "You're too much," the reason may be nonverbal, a simple habit of moving your legs far apart. Or the problem could be that you enthusiastically move your arms with very far-flung gestures.

Please don't cut yourself down to the size of someone who feels overpowered by you. For long-term happiness, you need a peer. Still, you might be willing to tame any ultra-wide gestures.

Now, what if you've started to feel invisible in your relationship, as though you don't leave any impression at all? Maybe it's time for you to **claim a bigger kinesphere.**

Add broader gestures. Especially add curved, arc-like motions with your arms. This can make your opinions seem extra authoritative.

Think about it. Timid, fidgety gestures shrink your kinesphere. For maximum clout, also avoid up-and-down arm movements... unless you're conducting an orchestra.

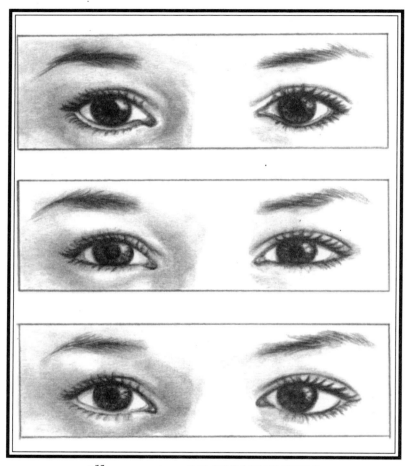

Illustration 15. WARINESS

Expect wariness of strangers to be inversely proportional to the curve in the lower half of the eye (a.k.a. lower eyelids).

+ With our pictures here, start from the top and read one eye at a time. They aren't identical, are they?
+ Each lower eyelid could be curvy, straight, or moderately curved. What do you find?

Turn the page for answers.

26. Loyalty

Will your partner stand by you through thick and thin (including any physical bouts with thinness and thickness)? Loyalty is one of the easiest qualities to read accurately. Remember, though, even the strongest loyalty won't last if you habitually criticize your partner.

BODY LANGUAGE

Protective gestures reveal the intent to love and care for you. A significant other may wrap an arm around your shoulder. Or while you're standing side-by-side, an arm, hand, leg or foot may unconsciously move into a position that symbolizes protectiveness.

Sometimes this protective component is exaggerated when posing for photos... all the better, as a public show of loyalty.

Eye contact shows loyalty, too. When you're among friends, does your partner look at you often? Loyalty shows as **attention sandwiches,** where your partner alternates looking at you with checking out the competition.

Having this eye gaze return is one way to distinguish friendliness from a roving eye, where happy hunting alternates with furtive, guilty, or reluctant glances back at you. By contrast, affectionate come-back-to-you looks, after interacting with other people, are more like the sweet filling in an Oreo.

FACE READING

Sure, you've gazed into your partner's eyes. But did you ever notice their shape on the bottom half? Make it your business to notice **lower eyelid curve.** It reveals so much about loyalty.

+ *Curvy lower eyelids* correspond to making friends quicker, but possibly dumping them quicker, too.

+ A *straight lower eyelid* means your partner may be hard to get to know, but will be intensely loyal once you become friends.
+ Moderate eyelid curve suggests a fine balance between openness and self-protection.

You can also revisit **jaw width** to learn about loyalty. (See Page 87.) *Wide jaws* bring great loyalty, at the price of stubbornness. A partner with *narrow* jaws is more likely to discuss problems in your relationship, but may be less willing to stick around if a conflict remains unresolved.

AURAS

Could you be an **energy holder?** About 1 in 20 people has a significant gift for holding, stabilizing and grounding energy for other people. Consider this loyalty at its finest. To learn who has it, begin with your usual Preparation Process. (See Page 25.)

Set an intention to learn the truth about this person. Plug in at the Timing databank at the Physical Chakra. Ask "How does this person hold energy for others?" Energy holders show a slow-moving pattern of energy at the root chakra. Clairvoyantly, you may perceive a lot of green, or symbols like roots. Whether or not your partner is an energy holder, everyone has fascinating inborn strengths at this databank.

Illustration 15. QUIZ ANSWERS

What did you make of the shape at each lower eyelid? From the top down, I found:

Curvy — Signalling maximum openness toward strangers.
Straight — Suggesting that all strangers will be tested.
Moderate on the right eye — Indicating moderate openness.
But did you notice? That final left eye also counts as **curvy.**

27. Lying

Think you can tell liars by their body language? Wrong. Even trained F.B.I. investigators are deceived half the time. The more polished the liar, the harder to spot that sheen. Fortunately, there are more reliable ways to tell who's lying than to use body language alone.

BODY LANGUAGE

Here are **the conventional tip-offs to lying** from nonverbal communication:

+ Sweating
+ Blinking faster than usual
+ Shifty gaze
+ Exaggerating a super-sincere look, furrowed brow, etc.
+ Rubbing or touching the nose
+ Talking extra fast
+ Changing tone of voice, or pitch, while telling the lie
+ Fidgeting, rocking back and forth, etc.
+ Licking the lips or running the tongue over teeth... the better to lie through them?

Here's why I hate depending on any of these cues. If the liar doesn't feel nervous, how many of these tip-offs will show? Zero.

Compulsive liars like fibbing.

Wicked people are more likely to jump for joy than look upset.

Troubled folks, with severe psychological problems, may feel dissociated from their misdeeds; twitches won't start to surface until the person cracks up completely.

Oy veh! The subject is dismal. On the bright side, once you have practiced reading auras, you'll never need to waste your time again, depending on these inferior ways to spot liars.

FACE READING

Some (not all) habits with lying show in faces. It's especially revealing to compare photos of the same person taken years apart. As a result of free will, every facial feature can change, and all facial changes have meaning.

For a quick study, here are the easiest danger signals to spot. Count them as especially ominous if they have become more extreme over the last five years.

A **crooked smile** indicates lying, either to self or others. Yeah, yeah. I know crooked smiles are sometimes considered oh-so-charming. Allow yourself to be charmed only if you also like to be deceived.

Equally troubling are **mouth pulls**. When the lips show a horizontal preference for one side of the face over the other, that's like the expression, "Talking out of one side of his mouth."

Especially worrisome is a mouth pull to the right. This suggests speech for public consumption, lacking in private conviction.

Ready for more mouth morsels? Compare the fullness of the upper and lower lips. An **extra-pouty lower lip** — at least twice as full as the upper lip — signals a gift for persuasiveness. Potentially there's a temptation to misuse such a gift, as in selling ice to Eskimos. (But remember, people with these lip proportions don't necessarily lie. Deception is just a potential challenge.)

Hooded eyes can be a problem. Physically, these eyes combine a deep set, well under the brow bone, with large eyelid thickness.

Hooded eyes may correspond to a capacity for guile. Or you could just be in the presence of someone who'll fall for you like a ton of bricks, treating you, the significant other, far better than anyone else in the world

Finally, notice a rare **eyelid asymmetry.** Have you ever seen someone with huge eyelid thickness on the right eye plus teensy eyelid thickness on the left? Hypocrisy alert!

Sure, anyone may dabble in hypocrisy, but folks with this eyelid combo can be pros. (Also, sometimes, cons.)

AURAS

Auras can reveal everything from chronic lying to temporary fibbing. Use these three simple **lie detector tests.**

Begin with your usual Preparation Process: Pay attention to your inner awareness, then Get Big and set the intention to learn truth dispassionately. (For more details, see Page 25.)

For **verbal veracity,** plug-in at the Verbal Integrity databank in the Communication Chakra. Ask, "What communication patterns show here?"

Deceptive actions require no verbal component. They can be worse than fibs. To protect yourself, plug-in at the Power Integrity databank at the Power Chakra and ask, "How does he/she use power?"

A final form of lying involves **spiritual authenticity.** More people than you might think habitually tell themselves that black = white. Find out by plugging into the Spiritual Integrity databank at the Spirituality Chakra. Ask "What's going on with his/her spiritual integrity?"

To master the delicate art of reading auras for deception, here is some recommended reading: *Empowered by Empathy,* pages 204-210, and *Aura Reading Through All Your Senses,* pages 139-140 and 147-148.

Finally, remember this law of nature. Remember it if you have discovered that your partner has a problem with lying. **Nature abhors a vacuum.**

So don't be afraid to create a space. If you're in a relationship with somebody you can't trust, say goodbye. Provided that you make every effort to be honest yourself, the Universe can supply a truthful new partner to fill the space you've created.

Gay or Straight?

Metrosexuals aren't the only people whose sexual orientation may seen confusing. Sure, you can read some cues from body language. But they're just as likely to mislead you... unless you're doing your research at a gay bar.

People lie to themselves about sex. They lie to others. And even if they aren't lying, reading a person's sexual orientation can be mighty confusing.

Straight men may appear effeminate because of how they present themselves. But guyliner (male eyeliner), manbags (male handbags) and mandals (dark leather, thick-soled sandals for men) are clothing choices, not proof of sexual preference.

Likewise, female clothing may tell you less than you think. If a woman avoids wearing skirts and favor short haircuts, so what?

What does clothing prove about sexual orientation? Zip! Watch out or you'll do the equivalent of complimenting a woman who is "obviously" pregnant. You know how it feels when, instead of being pleased, she glowers at you (or her belly) and growls, "That's no baby, it's fat."

Body language becomes somewhat more reliable as a way to read gay vs. straight when you've already started canoodling and your partner is turned off instead of on.

Unfortunately, that's a little late to find out. Besides, sexual orientation may not be the reason. The poor fool simply may not feel that you are his/her type.

Face reading won't tell you who's straight or gay, either. Still, male and female qualities affect more than intercourse. **Masculine-feminine balance** is one name for the sexual seesaw within every person.

- **Masculine energy** *is about doing, achieving, taking initiative, creating success one smart step at a time.*
- **Feminine energy** *is about being, attracting, learning from inner life, creating success by getting aligned inwardly, then taking congruent action.*

Ideally, each of us can balance both energies. In fact, anyone you know who is crazy desperate to get married probably has an equally urgent need... for more masculine-feminine balance.

Face reading can help you to understand more about this vital, but subtle, type of balance.

Every **straight** *shape on the face (chin, eyebrows, and everywhere in between) relates to an approach to life that could be considered "masculine" while* **curves** *could be considered "feminine."*

Angles *are the other main shape available and they signify "need to control," something you may have observed to be an equal opportunity human need. (Remember Page 99?)*

As you delve into physiognomy, you will find dozens, even hundreds, of physical traits, all of them rich with meaning. Regardless of how experienced you are so far, reading faces, you might find it especially interesting to study your own face for male-female balance.

Admittedly, researching this topic won't give conclusive proof of sexual orientation. You will, however, gain new appreciation for the complexity of gender.

Masculine and feminine qualities aren't a matter of either-or. Deeper inquiry will reveal a continuum, with exclusively male on one edge and exclusively female on the other. No place along that continuum guarantees sexual orientation.

Metrosexual, whatever-sexual... read people deeper. Don't just assume.

28. Money, Saving

Gee, do partners ever fight over money? Let me count the ways.

Wait, here's a better idea. Avoid problems by learning how both of you relate to saving. (Then turn to the next section of this book to learn about SPENDING, the other side of the coin.)

BODY LANGUAGE

Clothing is a nonverbal language rich in monetary insight. The *old money* pattern is to buy quality classics, like tweedy jackets or pearls, and wear them forever, suggesting an inclination to save. By contrast, the *nouveau riche* pattern is to buy flashy, trendy, disposable clothes.

Regardless of price point, read deeper. Sometimes a person simply hates buying new clothes and isn't otherwise a saver, while a date who impresses you with his/her new clothes may just be trying to impress you. Once you've been snagged, or snogged, he/she may never shop for clothes again. Scary as a wolf in sheep's clothing, a partner like this is a saver dressed up as a spender.

In the confusing realm of finance, it's common for people to misrepresent themselves without lying. A self-described financial conservative could be a profligate spender on hobbies. Stingy folk often think they're generous, and describe themselves accordingly. Clothing won't tell you everything, but I'd trust it more than talk.

FACE READING

Noses are an easy way to learn about financial patterns, with **nose tip size** directly correlated to saving style. To gauge this face data, dare to go frontal. Yes, stare at a schnozz straight on, neither up nor down but right on the level. Compare the relative sizes of nose tip, mouth and eyes; you also can compare nose tip size to the width of the nose ridge (i.e., the main part of the nose).

Chunky nose tips relate to a need for financial security. Here's someone who plans for the future and frets over the size of his/her nest egg. A bigger nose tip corresponds to a stronger need to save.

Petite nose tips suggest a lack of concern with financial security. Instead, there's a built-in prosperity consciousness. Since there will always be enough money, why plan?

Moderate nose tips correspond to sensible saving habits. The potential problem is assuming that this is the one and only way that everyone should deal with money.

AURAS

When talking money with your honey, don't just listen. Read chakras.

Begin with your usual Preparation Process: Pay attention to your inner awareness, then Get Big and set an intention to learn more about this person. (For more details, see Page 25.)

Plug-in at your partner's Financial Responsibility databank at the Physical Chakra and ask, "What is going on now with his/her relationship to money?"

You may be amazed how much information can result from such a simple question. Ask follow-up questions at will.

Weird monetary behavior can result from addictions. What if your partner has a secret problem with gambling, alcohol or drugs? This can be hidden from surface observers but not to you, reading the Physical Chakra.

Aura reading won't predict the full extent of erratic behavior, any more than the Richter Scale can measure an earthquake that hasn't happened yet. But at least you can learn if you're living near a fault line.

29. Money, Spending

Courtship behavior reveals precious little about how your lover normally spends money.

That trim, well-groomed, positive person who's trying to impress you is like a spic-and-span house newly put on the market, while his/her lived-in look may be completely different.

Protect yourself by reading cues to long-term spending patterns.

As for your work life, sure, reading this category could be useful, too. But supplement deeper perception by checking references, reading annual reports, calling the Better Business Bureau.

BODY LANGUAGE

Tipping in restaurants and taxis is revealing, including your partner's body language while the money is offered. Micro-expressions will cross his/her face. Will you find reluctance or warm-heartedness, mechanical calculation or tight-lipped resignation?

You can learn more from tipping behavior than from the presents your partner gives you.

Flowers and candy may be special treats reserved for courtship, whereas tipping reflects treatment of people who don't have to be impressed.

Someone who's kind to the help today will more likely be generous with *you* tomorrow.

In addition, generosity and stinginess show in apparently trivial **housekeeping purchases.** When you visit his/her house, head straight for the bathroom— at least to do your detective work.

Brands of soap, tissues, towels and other everyday items tell a lot about willingness to spend money on creature comforts.

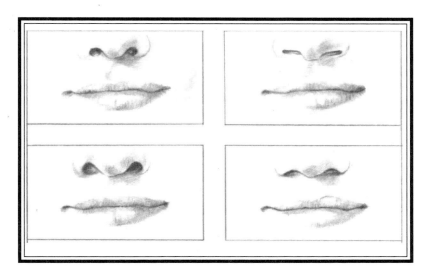

Illustration 16. Nostril Size and Shape

Go investigate, intrepid face reader!

First, note the **size** of nostrils here. They range from very large to very small.

Then see if you can match the nostril **shape** to its drawing. Here we have at least one of each:

- ◆ Rectangular nostril
- ◆ Triangular nostril
- ◆ Round nostril
- ◆ Flared nostril

For answers, turn the page.

FACE READING

To read long-term spending patterns, delve into nostrils. Don't be shy. Nostril size and shape supply valuable information.

Nostril size reveals *amount* of spending. Until you knew this was meaningful, you might not have noticed, but nostrils come in three sizes: *large, small* and *medium.*

Intrepid nasal detective, be sure to look on the level, neither up nor down. When nostrils show clearly, they are large. If you can't see the breathing holes, count them as small. The medium-sized nostril (Goldilocks' favorite) is right in-between.

Large nostrils signal generous spending. Small nostrils suggest frugality. And medium-sized nostrils can swing both ways.

Next, investigate **nostril shape,** which alerts you to *style* of spending. Granted, it may take some practice to focus on these cookie-cutter shapes, so you might want to start by reading your own nostrils in the mirror… preferably *not* while you're with your partner.

Again, remember to look on the level. You're paying attention to a shape sculpted in shadow, like the top half of a circle, tilted oval, box or triangle.

- *Round* nostrils curve into half-circles.
- *Flared* nostrils, the most common shape, are straight near the center of the nose but curve out extra toward the ear.
- *Rectangular* nostrils look like a box lid.

Illustration 16. QUIZ ANSWERS

Size: Large Shape: Round	Size: Small Shape: Rectangular
Size: Very large Shape: Flared	Size: Medium Shape: Right is round. Left is triangular.

· As for *triangular* nostrils, you'll see the apex of a triangle (although not the square on the hypotenuse).

Round nostrils correspond to enthusiastic spending. Frankly, folks with large, round nostrils are the biggest spenders on earth.

Flared nostrils mark adventurous spending, while rectangular nostrils suggest financial discipline, maybe even strict adherence to a budget.

Triangular nostrils reveal that someone has gone through painful experiences of scarcity, resulting in cautious spending.

Interpreting **asymmetries** with nostrils is simple. Just remember that data on the right side of a person's face relates to career while data on the left side relates to personal life.

Asymmetrical size or shape of nostrils shouldn't shock you. It just means that a person's life experiences have left their mark.

For instance, in Illustration 16, our final face showed a triangular nostril on the left only. This suggests that the woman endured some financial hardship that affected her personal life, rather than career. Before then, she probably had two round nostrils. After the trauma, her left nostril altered.

Not to shock you, I have had hundreds of conversations about nostrils. Time and again, I will describe the inner significance of nose data and ask for feedback. The owner of that particular nose will be impressed by the accuracy of the face reading.

What if nostril shape and size appear **contradictory**, as with large, triangular nostrils? Read that as financial conflict. Prepare to give your partner an extra measure of compassion.

AURAS

Screen your partner at the level of auras for truly nightmarish money problems: Financial deception, guilty secrets. Though answers won't be written in dollars and cents, questionable patterns will show.

Begin with your usual Preparation Process, (See Page 25.) Set an intention to learn freely, without expectations.

Plug-in at the Spending databank in the Physical Chakra and ask, "How does he/she handle money?"

For added protection from spending problems, initiate a conversation about money.

Besides paying attention to what your partner says, visually plug-in at the Verbal Integrity databank at the Communication Chakra and ask, "What is going on right now with truthfulness?"

How do You Spend Your Words?

*A highly productive way to read your partner involves **verbal transactions**. If words are money, how does your partner spend?*

Here I'll list 10 popular topics. Which is talked about most?

1. Emotions: Everyday dramas, problems and solutions

2. Creativity: Art, dance, film, music, novels, theater, TV

3. Health: Diet, illnesses, lifestyle choices, sports, weight

4. Ideas: Books and articles, classes, technology, theories

5. Money: Consumerism, cost, quality, shopping, social status

6. Physical life: Animals, cooking, exercise, nature, sports

7. Politics: News, activism, politicians, principles

8. Religion: God, energy, metaphysics, movements, scripture

9. Science: Discoveries, investigations, studies

10. Sex: Your relationships, other relationships; good bodies, bad bodies

Chances are, just a few topics dominate every conversation. Do these topics truly matter to you?

Gauge your partner's interest today in the topics that turn you on. Then, tomorrow, next year, next decade... your conversations will add up to a meaningful relationship.

30. NURTURING

Ooh, how about dating someone nurturing for a change? Does this sound completely uncool?

But wait. You could win big if you hook up with a partner who can give your *life* the equivalent of a full-body orgasm.

Maybe nurturing is important to you for work as well. But note that a big need to be nurtured at work may suggest that the more important business partner to read might be... you.

BODY LANGUAGE

Let's explore the two basic ways for a partner to look at you, stare or gaze. **Staring** is a display of masculine energy. Eye focus is strongly directed, purposeful and assessing. Your partner is *talking* through the eyes, rather than listening.

When he/she stares, it signals that awareness comes through the mind. Highly self-centered people will only stare, never gaze—assuming that they even bother to make eye contact.

Gazing is a display of feminine energy. Eyes appear softer, curious, receptive, inwardly alert. It's like *listening* through the eyes. Gazing shows that a love interest aims to connect to your heart and soul, not just your booty or your credit card.

Gazing takes time and awareness. Will he/she put down that cell phone to give you some undivided attention? You deserve that, especially if nurturing matters a lot at this time in your life. And even the strongest people need nurturing sometimes.

FACE READING

Degrees of kindness show in communication patterns, with nurturing at one extreme, cruelty at the other, and most human behavior falling somewhere in-between. To read tendencies in either direction, look where? **Lip bottoms.** That's right, examine the shape at bottom edge of the lower lip.

Usually, it's *curved.* If so, check out the degree of **lower lip curve.** Most people have some, meaning that their default manner of talking is moderately nurturing. But some people's lower lips show a very deep curve, which signals a special gift for supportiveness.

Occasionally, you'll find an *angled* lip bottom. That's good for leadership or the need to stay in control. Will nurturing be on the agenda? Maybe not.

Finally, you will sometimes encounter a *straight* lip bottom. However open that person's heart, the speech style is no-nonsense. While this can work well in business, personally you might want to put your guard up a bit. Someone who shoots straight from the lip can be nurturing, but it's more apt to show in actions than words.

AURAS

Nurturing can be read more accurately in auras than at any other level. Begin with your usual Preparation Process: Pay attention to your inner awareness, then Get Big and set an intention to be open and receptive to the truth. (For more details, see Page 25.)

Plug-in at the Nuturing databank in the Power Chakra, then ask questions like these:

 + "How does he/she show caring?"
 + "How does he/she handle my vulnerabily?"

Keep on researching databanks until a picture emerges of your partner's patterns around giving you support. Then, while you're at it, why not check out your own?

If your own nurturing abilities are so huge that you mostly give and seldom take, you're likely to attract a taker. But you can make that pattern history.

Re-train your friends by acting as your own advocate. Expect more, ask for more and you'll receive more. If you carry forth this pattern in your new relationships, you'll screen out friends who can't give to you in the way that you need.

Raise Your Social IQ

If only it were this easy to raise your *regular* intelligence quotient! **Emotional IQ** means the ability to recognize emotions and name them correctly. Score high and you're more likely to be popular. But even if you score low right now, don't be discouraged.

Most people just need a little practice to wake up this kind of intelligence. Soon you may join the ranks of the gifted and talented. Here are three different games, all fun.

Human Lotto

Remember Lotto, the kid's game with drawings of animals? That's where you try to match the correct name to each picture.

Even more thrillingly useful than being able to tell kangaroos from porcupines, why not play Human Lotto?

Find photos to read, whether from the Internet, a newspaper or your family picture album. Scrutinize the facial expression and body language. What does each person's picture say? Use emotional words like "Worried," "Angry," "Confused."

If you have trouble, that's because you haven't yet learned to recognize nonverbal language. Don't blame yourself. Maybe your parents were illiterate in this department. See if a friend can coach you.

This emotional Lotto can be funnier than a day at the zoo. After you or your coach names the emotion, both of you can take turns making up wild and wacky dialog for the person in the photo.

Produce Your Own TV

Watch a program without the sound. It's Social IQ TV, like a silent movie where you supply the dialogue. Don't tell a normal story. Describe emotions.

Sometimes a person has trouble reading emotions on a particular group of people:

- Attractive people of the **opposite** sex. Friends of the **same** sex.
- People the **age** of your parents or children.
- People with a different **skin** color.
- People who are **richer** than you. Or **poorer.**

Well, lucky you! There's sure to be a TV show about this very group of people. Find it. Watch it. With practice, you'll open your heart. "Sportscasting" during this game can help. Afterwards, emotions may always broadcast more clearly for you.

A Class Act

A person can have trouble with Social IQ due to carrying around old emotional pain. Psychotherapy or spiritual healing can help. But sometimes an acting class could do the trick, too.

Actors learn to supply **subtext,** having a hidden agenda or special set of emotions hidden just beneath the surface. Well let your subtext become a Social IQ Game.

The whole point of your performance will be expressing emotions. Display exactly one feeling per scene, whether you read lines, improvise, or do more formal acting. Inwardly, name each emotion. Also name every other actor's emotions.

Then, very important, debrief after every class. Call a friend or write in a journal. What did the acting and naming feel like to you? Discuss which emotions you liked or disliked, and why.

31. Power

The battle of the sexes — sure it's supposed to be about sex. As if! Power's more like it, most of the time.

Although reading your partner won't lift you above the battlefield, at least you can become a more educated warrior.

BODY LANGUAGE

Smile swapping is one cue to power balance. Which of you initiates most of the smiles and jokes? In body language, he who laughs last... holds the power.

No matter how eager you are for this relationship to work, don't throw your power away. The next time you and your partner meet, observe who smiles first. Unlike a shootout in the old West, the partner with *less* power tends to be quicker on the draw (and offers up the broader smile). Consciously change your performance and you may subtly improve your standing in the relationship.

Shocking but true: Unless you and your partner are reading this book together, you have the greater desire to understand your relationship. Probably you're also the one with less power. If so, why?

To re-evaluate power dynamics in your relationship, pay special attention to the body language of **deference**. Even if you don't bow to each other, Japanese-style, submissiveness can show in plenty of other ways. Does one of you physically look up to the other, tilting your head as well as aiming your eyes?

Of the two of you, whose gestures are less relaxed? Which of you unconsciously mirrors the other's position? Marking physical **territory** (a.k.a. kinesphere), does one of you move your legs, feet, arms or hands so that you take up less space than the other?

To complete your survey, take one more look from the neck up. Which of you nods more? Raises eyebrows more? Who gives more cute little grunts of acknowledgement? You know what this shows about power.

Well, defer when it serves you. Flatter that partner's ego, so long as *you* also get what you need from the relationship. Just don't settle for less.

FACE READING

Power shows in **cheek proportions.** Any style can be compatible with yours, provided that you and your partner acknowledge each other's right to have power in the relationship.

To develop your face reader's eye for power style, start with yourself. Compare the widest part of your face to its width at the cheeks. Below are the five major options in the power style category.

First, though, I might as well warn you about **asymmetry with cheek proportions.** It is quite common to have one style on the left, something else on the right.

Although I hesitate to bring up any extra complication, actually I am simplifying. A newbie will often try to match both sides of a face, shoving them into the same power style category.

That's more confusing than having you know, right from the outset, *not* to expect both sides of the face to show the same power style. You have one for personal life (left side) and one for career (right side). Use the illustration on the facing page to train your eye.

1. CHEEKS are the widest part of your face

You need to be the leader. When you and your partner are asked a question, you pipe up first. And secretly, or not so secretly, you prefer to be the center of attention.

What if both of you have the same cheek proportions? One still will be bossier than the other (probably the one whose cheeks stick out more) yet both of you must learn to share power.

Illustration 17. CHEEK ASYMMETRIES

Be brave, face readers. Take the extra second to check out each side of the face separately. Then name the cheek proportion style on each side.

+ Which cheek proportion shows on each face, each side?
+ How many of these faces shows symmetry with the cheek proportions?

For answers, turn the page.

It may help for each of you to supplement your time as a couple with times when you engage in other social relationships. There, each of you has the chance to shine (okay, dominate).

2. UNDER-CHEEKS are the widest part of your face.

That widest part counts whether it's fleshy cheeks or very wide jaws. Either way, you're a harmonizer. Having everyone get along matters so much that you'll bend over backwards to keep the peace.

Nevertheless, it's important to voice discontents when you have them. Otherwise, you'll act like "the rock" most of the time, bringing stability to others while stuffing your upset feelings. Explosive displays of temper can be the unintended, but inevitable, consequence.

3. THE FOREHEAD is the widest part of your face.

Only about 1 in 200 people has your power style, which is just as well, because you're so intense. Dynamism enables you to accomplish more than others. Still, until you credit yourself for having a talent, you may simply grumble that other people are lazy, which is not necessarily so.

And here's something even more surprising about your power style. To compensate for being intense, you may have cultivated the opposite kind of body language. Do you appear ultra-relaxed? In any room full of people, you're probably the one whose posture proclaims "Business casual." If they only knew!

4. YOUR WHOLE FACE is evenly wide.

Congratulations on having the polite power style. It's just as mixed a blessing as any of the other power styles, but at least you're more likely to come across as a nice person. Although you're great at working the system (any system) to produce results, you don't

Illustration 17. QUIZ ANSWERS

Unlike TV stars, real people have many asymmetries, including what shows in cheeks. For power style in a **work** partner, read the right side. For power style in a **personal** relationship, read the left side. All five faces here have asymmetrical cheeks.

+ **Top left:** Right, Cheek even; Left, Cheek widest
+ **Top right:** Right, Cheek widest; Left, Under-cheek widest
+ **Center:** Right, Cheek even; Left, Under-cheek widest
+ **Bottom left:** Right, Forehead widest; Left, Under-cheek widest
+ **Bottom right:** Right, Forehead widest; Left, Cheek even

necessarily call attention to yourself. The challenge is being over looked. So it's very important that you train your partner to praise you, early and often.

5. Your face is DIAMOND-SHAPED

Cheeks are widest, but your face tapers, both at forehead and jaws, the sign of a proven survivor. Your inner strength has been tested so often that you may find it hard to receive.

Why not let things be easy sometimes? Accept that compliment, not to mention other trinkets of affection that your partner gives you. Sure, you're probably used to having to do every blasted thing for yourself. But you have a partner now, remember?

AURAS

To protect your personal power, plus the overall health of your aura, defend yourself against **psychic coercion.**

This common problem is unleashed whenever one person outlines how another adult's life should appear, e.g., "You're dressing all wrong," or "How come you're not married yet? You should get married."

When someone repeatedly sends you a message that you should dress a particular way, act a particular way, produce a particular number of offspring, etc., laugh it off if you can.

Coerciveness happens, but if you're inwardly strong it won't get to you. Otherwise, you may take on the psychic equivalent of dust bunnies. And bunnies like this aren't cute, especially when they're stuck in your aura by the truckload.

While it may take a session with a trained spiritual healer to fully clean out the problem, you can start protecting yourself from this kind of power struggle with one simple choice: Pray for the will to recognize — and follow — your own true desires.

32. Problem Solving

Everyone has a good side. Reading deeper, you can find it... then use it as your built-in resource for problem solving.

BODY LANGUAGE

Should the two of you start to argue, listen to your partner's breathing. **Deeper breathing** will help him/her to relax enough to hear your point of view.

For a subtle trick of body language that encourages this, deliberately synchronize your breathing with your partner's. Inhale and exhale at his/her present tempo. Once you're both in synch, gradually deepen your breath, moving into a slower rhythm.

Now **pace your voice.** As you speak, slow down the pace of your words to match your breath. Continue until your partner entrains to your tempo. Patience, please. It won't help to push things along by barking out commands like, "Calm down."

When your partner's breathing has relaxed to match your own, problem solving will come easier.

FACE READING

Although nothing on a face is necessarily bad, eight physical characteristics can warn you of potential problems. Here they are, plus what to do about them.

1. FINE EYELASHES
These lashes are either sparse or thin-textured or both.
Problem: Hair-trigger temper (the flip side of sensitivity).
+ Don't criticize your partner's highly sensitive reactions. Validate them instead.

2. PUFFS OVER EYES

A puff is a swollen area between brow bone and upper eyelid. (See Page 114. The woman's right eye has a puff.)
Problem: Crankiness expresses as irritability over small things.
+ Make concessions early in the argument. Otherwise your partner's peevishness may escalate.

3. VERY FULL EYEBROWS WITH A DEEP ANGLE

The eyebrow is well endowed, and its shape includes a hinge place where the hair changes direction. (See the man's right eyebrow on Page 52.)
Problem: Constant evaluation of what's said and done. No qualms about confronting a "wrongdoer."
+ Hold your ground, if necessary, but don't resist, not unless you're spoiling for a fight.

4. MACHO KNOB

This is a doorknob-like circle of raised muscle at the bottom of the chin.
Problem: Temper linked to masculine pride, or a woman's pride in her partner.
+ Love the sexiness, if not the angry outburst.

5. GOATEE OR ANGLED CHIN BOTTOM

A goatee is a beard with a triangular shape. (See an angled chin bottom on the first illustration, Page 99.)
Problem: Control freak tendencies in this person may emerge when you display a will of your own
+ Either stay submissive or hide your independence.

6. TWO CLOSE-SET EYES

Eyes are less than one eye's width apart. (See the center illustration on Page 89.)

Problem: A talent for perpetual criticism
+ Try changing the subject. You may be able to divert an equal-opportunity criticizer.

7. ONE FAR-SET EYE + ONE CLOSE-SET EYE

As always, look at one side of the face at a time. Reading eye set, sometimes you'll find this combination. On Page 183, all five faces have a close-set eye on the left. In addition, both women have a far-set eye on the right.

Problem: Unpredictable criticism as he/she swings from easygoing to hard-to-please
+ Learn to recognize your partner's two different modes. Discuss controversial topics when the easygoing side prevails.

8. BLADE-SHAPED LOWER LIP

This rare mouth configuration is long, with a lower lip that tilts inward. Shape, overall, is wider in the center than at the edges.

Problem: Insults are sarcastic, cold, and way too accurate.
+ End the conversation, resuming when your partner's mood has passed. Also, never initiate bickering, because your partner may quickly escalate to verbal cruelty.

AURAS

Some chakras within a person's aura can be disproportionately large. These are strengths. When you need to solve problems, appeal to the areas of life symbolized by those **bigger chakras**. Begin research with your usual Preparation Process. (See Page 25.) Set the intention to compare chakra proportions.

Plug-in at one chakra at a time. Ask, "How important is this aspect of life to him/her now?" Explore, in turn, the Physical, Sexual, Power, Emotional, and Spiritual Chakras.

Depending on which chakra is biggest, favor the corresponding aspect of life when you talk with your partner:

+ Common sense for a big Physical Chakra,
+ Sexy talk for a big Sexual Chakra
+ Discussion of ideas and concepts for a big Power Chakra
+ Acknowledgement of feelings for a big Emotional Chakra
+ Your shared belief system (or the closest you can come) for a big Spiritual Chakra.

For instance, "I don't want to go to the soccer game because...

+ "I'd rather stay home and turn our bed into a sports arena."
+ "Watching either team lose will make me upset."
+ "I'm more drawn to Bible study. Care to join me? "

Blow off Problems

When you blow out all the candles on a birthday cake, that's supposed to make wishes come true. But why wait until your next birthday to use your breath to solve problems?

Here's a powerful technique you can use any time you like, including un-birthdays. Just one catch: It looks funny. So do it in front of your roommate, not your partner.

Give yourself five minutes, and breathe through your left nostril only. To make that happen, gently push your right thumb against your right nostril.

Now that you've found the spot, close your eyes, relax, and breathe in and out through the open side of your nose for a full five minutes.

This technique is guaranteed to calm you down. Why? According to the ancient wisdom of yoga, each nostril has a specialty that affects your energy. The right nostril adds energy, like the sun. The left nostril brings serenity, like the moon.

Just a few minutes of moonlight breathing can make you surprisingly mellow.

33. RELIGION

Unless religion is your life, don't discuss it during a first meeting with anyone. And never discuss religion at work. Unless religion is your business, it's none of your business.

But friendships and love relationships are different. As you and a partner draw closer together, questions about your beliefs will arise. Still, how much will mere words tell you? Some mixed marriages work better than same-faith pairings.

Besides, during the course of a long-term relationship, a person's faith can change, whether this change is announced or not

These are just some of the reasons why you may wish to read religion deeper. Investigate how both of you believe what you *say* that you believe.

BODY LANGUAGE

Although **jewelry** may seem like the ultimate nonverbal way to display religious affiliation, appearances can deceive.

Size matters — not penis size in this case but how huge the cross (or other symbol). Never equate large, conspicuous jewelry, or religious slogans on a tee shirt, with closeness to God. The opposite is more likely.

Jewelry size can reveal fear or be mostly a social display, proclaiming one's need to be seen as belonging to a religion. Read deeper to learn about genuine religious experience.

FACE READING

Proportions of an ear can speak volumes about religion. Check out your partner's **ear circle proportions.** Read the left ear for personal partnership, right ear for business relationship. Note the relative

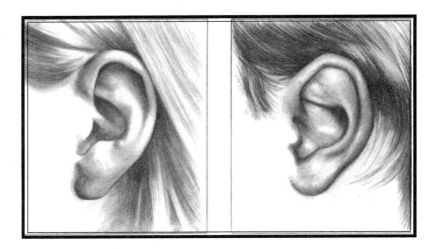

Illustration 18. EAR CIRCLES

Compare the relative sizes of the inner and outer ear circles.
- In our first illustration, the **outer** circle takes up more space.
- For our second illustration, the **inner** circle is larger.

---

sizes of both ear circles. Okay, they are actually half-circles. I've yet to meet someone whose ear makes a complete wheel shape.

Apart from this half-circle business, ear circles are not what most people notice about ear structure. Instead we focus on earlobes. *Earlobes* are located beneath both the ear circles.

- The *inner circle* is the deep area close to the ear hole, often looking as though it was fashioned with a cookie cutter.
- Separated from it by a semi-circular border of flesh lies the *outer circle,* which extends all the way from the top of the ear down to right above the earlobe.

What matters here? Notice the relative sizes of these two ear circles. Which is bigger, which smaller? Or are they equal?

A larger outer ear circle suggests that your partner is especially interested in religion's social benefits. Rituals may be important, too.

A larger inner ear circle suggests that your partner cares more about the spirit of the law than the rules.

Equally proportioned inner and outer circles mean that deep inclinations could go either way. Depending on context, outer might matter more than inner, or the reverse. To learn more, read....

AURAS

The truth about religion shows especially well at the Spirituality Chakra. Begin detective work with your usual Preparation Process: Pay attention to your inner awareness, then Get Big and set an intention to be open to new insights about this person. (For more details, see Page 25.)

Then plug-in at the Spiritual Growth databank in the Spirituality Chakra. Ask, "What's going on now with his/her spiritual life?"

Sometimes you'll find a big glow, signaling the active experience of spiritual source.

Some devout spiritual seekers even have Divine Beings lodged right at this chakra. For example, I found Francis of Assisi in the third eye of one man who, I later learned, kept a certain saint's statue right in his front yard. Jesus, Mary, Buddha, Shiva, and Krishna are some of the other beings I've found in clients' third eyes, using the technique described here.

An equally big surprise awaits when reading auras of people who make a big show of their piety. Usually that aura shows tiny spiritual experience, or none at all. Instead, the big part is about a sense of righteousness, fear, pain, or the urge to coerce other people.

Can that change? Sure. One simple prayer, from the heart, could do it. But never base a relationship on how your partner *could* improve. You'll be happier with someone compatible for you now.

Whether your spiritual connection is large or small, choose someone similar. This has nothing to do with social performances.

Auras are made of pure spiritual truth. Trust what they tell you.

34. Resentment

Surely the delights of resentment are overrated. What else can explain its popularity?

Whether your partner's target is you or somebody else, resentment can hurt your relationship. Usually the problem results from ignoring anger, so there can be a crying (or yelling) need for more assertiveness. Another cause of resentment is chronic blaming, a cheap substitute for taking personal responsibility when problems arise.

Blaming can hurt you, even if no reproachful words are spoken.

Yes, resentment is that sneaky. Read yourself for it, not just your partner, because an otherwise self-aware person can unknowingly harbor huge resentment. But it need not remain a deep, dark secret, not when you can use deeper perception.

BODY LANGUAGE

Before resentment goes chronic, it will show in micro-expressions. (See Page 9.) Later, you may find the same expressions held for extra-long — martyr-style — so you could notice "if you really cared." Hinting is not a highly effective way to bring up problems; still, this indirect method remains a perennial favorite.

Productive or not, the body language of serious resentment will often be shown behind your back. So I recommend that you use the Resentment Checklist that follows.

None of the "20 Ways" on our next page *proves* resentment, but any one of them gives you the relationship equivalent of a search warrant.

Ask, "Are you upset about something?" Then, whatever your partner answers, check out body language. You can even think of the following checklist as a nonverbal form of the game "20 Questions."

20 Ways to Spot Resentment

1. Veins or wrinkles, not usually seen, show on the *forehead,*
2. *Eyebrows* descend or angle downwards.
3. *Eyes* avoid you.
4. *Eyes* tell you "Duh!" by rolling in disgust.
5. While you're speaking, his/her *eyes* narrow.
6. While you speak, an *ear* or *nose* is rubbed.
7. The *mouth* position becomes unnatural, e.g., Lips tighten.
8. A mouth-only *smile* doesn't part the lips
9. Hands cover the *mouth.*
10. *Cheeks* are rubbed or sucked in.
11. *Jaws* tense.
12. *Chin* thrust changes, held more *out* or *in* than normal.
13. *Beard* is pulled or rubbed.
14. Unusual *twitches* show on any part of the face.
15. *Head* hangs.
16. Arms cross at *chest* level. (Emotions seems threatened).
17. Arms cross at *solar plexus.* (Power seems threatened).
18. Hands are folded in *lap.* (Sexual shut-down).
19. Turn-off shows in a physical turning away: *Head, shoulder, arm, hand, chest, knee, foot.*
20. *Voice* drops to a mumble.

FACE READING

You have already learned to read Anger Flags, a sign of hidden anger. (See Page 52.) They are vertical lines that go upward from the start of an eyebrow.

A fascinating hybrid line starts as an Anger Flag but then shifts toward the middle of the forehead. This **Sublimation Line** suggests that resentment has been channeled into a deeper commitment to spiritual life.

Dimples can hide resentment. Whether the permanent-press variety (ever-present on a cheek) or peek a boo dimples (round dots that appear only with a smile), both types correspond to fabulous talent for charming people. (See Page 74.)

Sometimes, however, dimples mask resentment. To spot an **angry dimple,** develop an eye for whether the cheek flesh near the dimple looks hard or soft. (Yes, with practice you can tell. Then you'll become wary of a dimple hard-on.)

AURA READING

Do you believe it is noble to stiff-upper-lip your way through life, carrying resentment? Aura reading may change your mind. Resentment there shows up as dead zones, parts of an aura bound up so tight that vitality no longer flows.

Holistic physicians have found the short-term consequences of resentment are depression and fatigue, while long-term effects may include cancer, diabetes and gallstones.

Could that be happening to you or your partner? Investigate, starting with your usual Preparation Process. (See Page 25.) Set the intention to open your heart to this person. Plug-in to the Problem-Solving databank at the Emotional Chakra and ask: "What's going on with emotions, long-term?"

Next, plug-in at the Problem-Solving databank at the Sexual Chakra. Ask: "What patterns show here?"

Finally, at the Conflict Resolution databank at the Power Chakra, ask: "What's going on here with empowerment vs. victimization ?"

However nobly motivated, resentment is toxic. By the time it shows in an aura, resentment cries out for healing, and the sooner, the better. Medical risks aside, inner numbness sucks the fun out of relationships.

You did get involved in this relationship to live *happily* ever after, right?

35. Respect

When your partner pays attention to you, doesn't that equal respect? Maybe not. While sampling the latest fad in lattes, he/she pays attention, too.

True respect is worth researching for a quality long-term relationship, or even for leaving a short-term one with dignity intact.

Research this category on yourself, too. If people would count respect points instead of calories or carbs, we'd have a far more beautiful society. Instead, many of us ignore the issue... until we have to reach for a tissue.

In work and personal life, both, you'll attract partners who treat you with as much respect as you subconsciously give yourself. Even if the two of you don't start off with a hand-in-glove fit, over the years you'll develop it. So make it good.

BODY LANGUAGE

How do you show respect at a play or concert? You applaud at the end. Well, in real life that happens too, just nonverbally.

So notice **exit behavior.** If your partner has approved of your performance at the meeting, party, restaurant, etc., it will be reflected in a graceful, respectful dance as you leave. Stiff body language can signal disrespect.

Leaning is inevitable, when two people leave a room. Respect shows when part of his/her body angles toward you. When hips, feet or other body parts angle away from you, how good a sign is that?

Respect Detectives, **eye contact** is your final way to read finales. As you exit the room, does your partner glance at you periodically? Or does he/she spring away at the soonest opportunity, as if freed from jail?

FACE READING

Each strong **facial contrast** between the two of you represents a chance for greater respect. Initially, you'll be fascinated by behavior that corresponds to your facial differences.

At work or play, opposites attract... for about six months. Afterwards, one of you may start to dislike—and thus stop respecting—precisely what set off your initial attraction.

For example, say Ms. Starter Eyebrows hooks up with Mr. Ender Eyebrows. Physically, this means that her eyebrows are fuller at the start, near the nose. His are fuller at the end (near an ear). (For starters, see the right eyebrow of Wary Woman, all three drawings on Page 162. Anger Flag Man on Page 52 shows one ender.)

This eyebrow category relates to different kinds of creativity while working on projects. She'll be stronger as an originator whereas he'll excel as an implementer.

What happens, respect-wise, when they work together? Initially she'll admire his fabulous follow-up with details while he'll adore her inventiveness. Deeper into the relationship, they may respond less to strengths and more to the other one's challenges.

"Suddenly" it seems like a big deal to her that Mr. Ender procrastinates before starting any new project, no matter how small.

And he begins grumbling because Ms. Starter's terrific projects often amount to nothing, being dropped halfway due to lack of interest. Especially for someone who prides himself on always nailing details, might that be a bit annoying?

To guard against this kind of disillusionment, it could help to share some friendly face reading. Discuss the meaning of your biggest facial contrasts. Joke about your differences before they become annoying. Later, remind yourselves as needed that each facial difference goes with a valuable talent in life, not just a potential challenge.

Ideally, partners show each other different ways to be. This can become a form of vicarious experience lived through your partner.

Sure, you'll be surprised sometimes, when he/she instinctively acts in a way that's completely different from yours. With perspective, however, vive la difference!

But perspective that interprets differences with respect is always a choice.

AURA READING

Do you really want to know the deep truth about respect in your relationship? Then do the aura reading equivalent of **before-and-after pictures.**

While the two of you are first together, do your usual Preparation Process. See Page 25. Set an intention to learn about your partner. Visually plug-in at the Respect databank in the Emotional Chakra. Ask, "What's happening emotionally?" Notice what you get.

Now, forget about auras. Engage fully in your conversation. Then, after you've been together for 15 minutes or more, repeat the previous steps of research.

Increased boredom, anger, or resentment are danger signs. Without referring to reading auras, you can ask about your interaction, e.g., "I sense that you're bored. Have you had a tough day?" Then do what you can to work out the problem.

Truth is, negativity in your partner may have nothing to do with you. But if it increases whenever you're together, chances are that you're habitually being blamed or disrespected.

That's especially likely if your partner isn't in touch with feelings and, therefore, transfers emotions from elsewhere and projects them onto you. His/her anger about work isn't really your fault. Discussion may call attention to the pattern so it can be changed.

By contrast, when a relationship goes well, you'll find that the state of your partner's Emotional Chakra *improves* after you've been together. This feel-good reaction will result in your being treated with respect.

36. Risk Taking

In the great manicure of life, some of us demand the emery board with coarse grain while others flinch from the least bit of roughness. Learn how much risk you prefer, in yourself, in a partner.

BODY LANGUAGE

Risk taking shows clearly in your partner's behavior behind the wheel. Clark Kent can turn into Superman, or the reverse. Body language when **driving a car** tells you plenty about aggression, temper, timidity and balance. Does this person even bother to follow the rules of the road?

Big risk-takers can scare the seat belts off low risk-takers, and not just in a car. Behavior behind the wheel can be played out later with work, money, career, health, you name it.

If you're a big risk taker, an unadventurous partner will bore you silly. (The religion of risk may have many missionaries but few converts.)

For more than a romantic romp, avoid pairing off with an extreme opposite. At work, similar styles matter even more.

Speaking of knowing what you're in for, **signaling behavior** from a driver is especially revealing. Careful communication tells you something altogether different from the "Why bother?" method.

Big risk takers who don't signal can make thrillingly spontaneous partners. But only you know how much thrill is too much.

And while you're in your partner's car, check out the decor. What do you find by way of neatness or clutter? How do you like the personal touches?

Décor like that moldy rabbit's foot may well festoon your living room one day. How do you like *that* risk?

FACE READING

When facing up to your partner's preferences for risk taking, **chin length** reveals most about personal style. (See a very long chin on Page 114, the lady on the lower left. For a very short chin, see Page 99, the middle drawing on the upper row.)

+ A *long chin* shows potential for physical courage and, potentially, recklessness. Another potential problem is lack of concern for ethics, resulting in a different kind of risk.
+ By contrast, a *short chin* suggests that your partner's courage tends to be ethical rather than physical. He/she will dare to do what's right, regardless of what others think. But so you seek physical chutzpah? Don't count on it.
+ Fortunate are the folks with *mid-length chins,* equally comfortable taking risks or not. Their challenge is judging the "crazies" at either extreme.

AURAS

What is your partner willing to die for? Everyone has an area of life where he/she will take special risks, be they physical, emotional or spiritual. To investigate the tradeoffs, read databanks corresponding to these three areas of life.

Aura reading will also enable you to contrast deep forms of courage — gifts of the soul — with fear or other blockage. Someone who has risked and lost big may turn timid, resentful, even impotent.

But remember, STUFF like this in an aura can always be healed. Your insights may set that in motion, depending upon what you find and whether you're willing to risk a tactful discussion.

Begin with your usual Preparation Process: Pay attention to your inner awareness, then Get Big and set an intention to open your heart and learn about this person. (For more details, see Page 25.)

Plug-in first at the Physical Courage databank in the Physical Chakra. Ask, "How does he/she relate to taking physical risks?"

Plug-in next at the Emotional Courage databank in the Emotional Chakra. Ask, "How does he/she relate to taking emotional risks?"

Finally, plug-in at the Spiritual Courage databank in the Spiritual Chakra. Ask, "How does he/she relate to taking ethical risks?"

Personally, I've found this kind of research to be surprisingly helpful. Here's how I first discovered it.

On a lovely Sunday afternoon, I was stuck in heavy Washington traffic, and I do mean thoroughly stuck. To pass the time, I started to read my aura.

What I found at the Physical Chakra was that part of me actually preferred driving at a crawl, due to a loathing for physical risks.

Contrast came at the emotional and spiritual chakras, where I proved to be an enormous risk taker, loving to evolve at racecar speeds.

Then came my aha! "Some folks are just the opposite. When their approach is slo-go, instead of feeling impatient, I could remind myself: 'Hey, kiddo. That is just how you *drive*.'"

Consequently, I'm kinder. When you examine your own risk-taking proclivities, maybe you, too, will score some useful insights.

37. Romance

How much romance do you need? Some of us do have a minimum daily requirement for Vitamin R, and it's high. We crave the tender look, the sweet surprise.

Since first dates won't necessarily reveal a partner's long-term need for romance, inquiring minds have two choices. Either drag out a crystal ball, imploring it to give you an accurate prediction, or find out what you need to know right now. Romance is one of the easiest categories to read at the levels of body language, face and aura.

BODY LANGUAGE

Length of eye contact provides your first clue. Which do you think needs more Vitamin R, someone who lingers over the sight of you or the pal who catches your eye with a quick "Hey" and "has it handled"?

Gesture height reveals even more. Hand movements that accompany talking can be made at different levels, corresponding to parts of the body. Are they made mostly *at the heart?* That points to an ever-expanding emotional life, directly related to Vitamin R.

Gestures *in the solar plexus* suggest intellectual focus.

And dare we consider the rare individual whose favorite gesture height is *crotch-level?* Don't expect him/her to pause for romance beyond what's required to bag you.

How many times have you seen public speakers fold their hands right there? So be aware that the grand exception to gesture height is **crossing gestures**, which include *folded hands* as well as *clutched elbows.*

Crossing symbolizes resistance to the corresponding area of life. Thus, the public speaker with hands folded right in front of the sex chakra says nonverbally, "Whatever you notice about me, puhleeze, don't let it be that I have sexual organs."

Alas, the partner with arms folded across the chest is saying nonverbally, "What romance? Are you kidding?" Forget about entering here unless you know how to pick a lock."

FACE READING

Eyebrow shape counts, whether the brows have been tweaked, plucked or sketched in with pencil. (See illustration at Page 99.) For clues to love relationships, pay special attention to the left brow.

Curved eyebrows indicate a high emotional IQ. This augurs well for romance. Let your partner know how important romance is to you and expect to receive plenty of Vitamin R.

Straight eyebrows suggest a fascination with ideas. Romance may be expressed in talk more than words. To encourage repeat performances, praise your partner's cleverness at speaking Cupid (and don't expect love in the form of flowery sentiment).

Angled eyebrows correspond to intellectual detachment. Typically the thinker observes, evaluates, and corrects.

The way to bring in romance is to emphasize creative control, as with a movie director who takes pride in setting up scenes. Express admiration at your partner's romantic achievements, emphasizing their creativity.

Another plus for romance is a **far-set left eye.** (See it illustrated at Page 99, top left.) Here's someone with a broad perspective, someone who dreams outside the box. True, a partner like this won't necessarily be the most practical partner but that's your trade-off for finding a born romantic.

AURAS

Imagine that you attend a one-room schoolhouse where all the grades are mislabeled. That's life here at Earth School. Our status labels have no bearing on spiritual life. One of the best ways to prove this to yourself is to compare people by reading their Physical Chakras

Some folks live in a jungle. Others inhabit a gray landscape that might be called "Boredom World." Maybe your partner lives in fairyland, an art museum, or the equivalent of a globe-sized amusement park. Whatever basic way of relating to life shows in this chakra, it's key to understanding his/her view of romance.

So read that the aura databank I call "Version of Reality." Begin with your usual Preparation Process: Pay attention to your inner awareness, then Get Big and set an intention to experience your partner's version of reality. (For more details, see Page 25.)

Plug-in at the Physical Chakra and ask, "How does he/she relate to physical life?"

Be prepared to find something very different from what's in your own aura. Root chakra patterns are as distinctive as a thumbprint. Therefore, each of us develops a unique way to be romantic. Through speech, actions, and touch, you and your partner can express the best that both of your worlds have to offer.

11 Ways to Enhance Romance

Yes, your use of **eye contact** can upgrade your love life.

1. To **gaze,** *switch on a soft, appreciative look, like the wide-angled lens of a camera. Not only will you put your lover at ease, but you'll signal your appreciation and help move the conversation into a timeless, romantic realm.*

2. To **stare,** *let your eyes focus hard, like the zoom feature of a camera. Want to make your lover squirm? You just might. For good or bad, your conversation will become more intense. Sometimes this builds up sexual tension.*

3. *It can be sexy to* **alternate,** *provided that you get the sequence right. Stare to catch your partner's attention, then soften to a gaze.*

4. *A prolonged gaze signals the amount of your involvement.* **Where** *on the body you look will signal the nature of your interest. Let the beholder beware. (See Page 118.)*

5. *Frequently alternate brief gazes with looking away. Ta da, you're flirting! Even a baboon would eventually respond to the pattern. (Make that* **especially** *a baboon. Our evolutionary ancestors reproduce too, you know.)*

6. *Another way to amp up your eye appeal is to use* **eyelash power.** *Blink languorously, as if your eyelashes have turned into a very large, heavy erogenous zone.*

7. *During a romantic encounter, don't expect that your partner's eye gaze will automatically increase. As your exchange grows more intimate, it's romantic for eye contact to actually* **decrease.**

8. *When a couple is* **in synch,** *you'll do the same amount of gazing. But if things aren't going so well, one of you will increase the gazing while the other does just the opposite. Take the hint.*

9. *By* **refusing** *to gaze, you can let a loser down gently.*

10. *But don't* **avoid eye contact** *completely, even if you're angry. It's like giving your partner the silent treatment. Nonverbally, you'd be denying your lover's existence.*

For better results, use words to communicate why you're upset and what you would like to change.

11. *Stares can be powerful for reinforcing a negative message, so* **don't do overkill.** *Ever hear a parent who's scolding a child say, "Look at me. Don't do blah, blah, blah. Understand?"*

Locking eyes like that may help with parenting but, for a romantic relationship, "scolding stares" can be the kiss of death.

38. Satisfaction

"I can't get no satisfaction" may be your partner's theme song. If it's your song, too, both of you could harmonize for a good long time, maybe even as long as the Rolling Stones!

Alternatively, you could make beautiful music together as ardent optimists. For compatibility, what matters is that both of you sing off the same sheet of music.

Otherwise what happens? As a yea-sayer, you may constantly feel dragged down by a nay-sayer. It's just as bad if the imbalance goes the other way.

Still, the ever-gurgling spring of hope is popular for good reason. Love — or a great work relationship — can triumph against bad odds. And maybe it will help you that satisfaction is one of the easiest things to read. Investigate two different levels at least. Then your inquiry (if not your partner) will leave you thoroughly satisfied.

BODY LANGUAGE

Smiles signal satisfaction, sure. But how much? Read smiles, emphasizing your partner's degree of engagement.

Does your partner smile with lips only? Then, sad to say, engagement is puny.

With full engagement, lip movements will be strong enough to move cheeks upward, plus his/her eyes will crinkle and flash with an extra sparkle. In general, greater engagement correlates with willingness to feel satisfaction.

It's a special plus if someone opens up with such a big grin that you can see both rows of teeth. Read this as exceptional engagement.

But what about **follow-through** after a smile? This can be as revealing as a tennis player's stroke after hitting the ball. When lips finish their social gesture, what happens? With strong follow-through, you'll know that satisfaction circuits are working fully.

+ Do eyebrows flash? (That's a fast rise-and-fall that shows intellectual interest)
+ Do eyes linger tenderly?
+ Do eyelashes bat flirtatiously?
+ Do pupils dilate sexily?
+ It's also encouraging if, post-smile, the lips pout or part. And special congratulations are due if previously clenched jaws relax.

Okay, now the smile has been read, also the follow-through. But don't stop your intrepid expression reading. What about **post-smile animation?**

With satisfaction, your partner's all-around liveliness increases after a smile, whereas a dissatisfied smile is followed by... a big fat nothing.

The extra liveliness of animation can show in a variety of ways, especially *expressiveness* (a strong projection of personality through the face) and *mobility* (fast-changing expressions, e.g., teasing, playfulness, showing off with eyelashes).

Oh, the complicated fun of body language! Your smile research isn't done yet. Turn attention now to your partner's **smile shockwaves.**

After the smile, what happens *below* the mouth? Does body language reach out to you? Comparing before and after the smile, has your partner's posture changed?

When you and your partner stand, positive shockwaves would be:

+ Head tilts sideways
+ Chin moves up or down
+ Shoulders round or straighten
+ And that special sign of approval, a chest swing or pelvis turn toward... you. (Oh, did you think of that even more

special sign of approval that men can give? Yes, that would count, not that any savvy partner would be caught starting.) If both of you are *sitting*, smile shockwaves can include a torso twist in your direction or a leg shift towards you.

As smile shockwaves go, this kind of subtle foot move is just as encouraging as, and arguably more tasteful than, a game of footsie.

What's so important about these smile shockwaves? Any one of them means that your partner has moved satisfaction from the face alone (a head trip about happiness) to include the body (which can involve the whole person and, on a good day, maybe even sex).

Remember the Cheshire Cat from *Alice in Wonderland*, with its disembodied smile that lingered? In a partner, you'd hope for more.

When a partner interacts with you as a whole person, you're more likely to give and receive complete satisfaction.

By contrast, sometimes a partner will send shockwaves without bothering to smile first. Count that as pure sexual come-on.

In a sexy movie, that's fun to watch. In real life, question it. That unsmiling partner is undoubtedly using you for sex. Do you want to be satisfied only from the neck down?

FACE READING

All those satisfaction pointers you've learned how to read only reveal short-term mood. To read long-term satisfaction, I recommend that you study **mouth angles.**

This face reading category is ultra-easy to read. In fact, depending on your purpose, you only need to read half a mouth. For job satisfaction, that's the right side. For love relationships read on the left.

Wait until your partner's lips are in repose (not smiling, talking, scolding, or kissing you). From the front, on the level, imagine a dot at the horizontal center of the mouth, right between the lips. Imag-

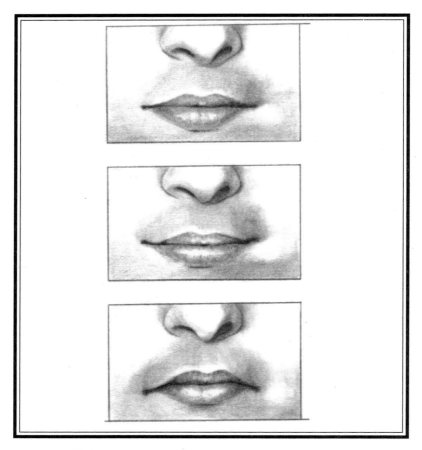

Illustration 19. MOUTH ANGLES

Oh this research is subtle, subtle but satisfying. Figure out which mouth angle is:

+ Up-angled,
+ Down-angled,
+ Even-angled

I do want to remind you, whenever you read faces or auras, to look on the level. If you're not holding this book up, for instance, your results will be distorted. And, of course, turn the page for answers.

ine a second dot at the leftmost corner of the mouth. Connect these dots with an imaginary line. Does it go down, up, or straight?

Most folks are *down-in-the-mouth.* This develops after having been hurt by unkind remarks. On the positive side, knowing how much words can hurt may lead to considerateness.

Thus, a slightly down-angled mouth can be an excellent thing to find in your partner. Extreme down-angling, however, suggests a low satisfaction quotient.

Up-angling signifies uncommon satisfaction, though not necessarily great sensitivity as a communicator. Teasing words from that mouth may hurt your feelings, especially if your own mouth angles down.

An *even-angled* mouth speaks of moderate satisfaction — without a tendency to tease.

AURAS

Both short-term and long-term satisfaction are *most* reliably read in an aura. Start with databanks about your partner's attitude toward life in general at the Physical Chakra.

Use your usual Preparation Process. (See Page 25.) Set an intention to learn about this person's patterns with satisfaction. Plug-in at the Reality databank at the Physical Chakra and ask, "What's going on now with his/her view of life?"

Then plug-in at the Satisfaction databank in the Emotional Chakra and ask, "What's happening now with his/her satisfaction?"

Ask follow-up questions, at either databank, about past experiences, gifts, problems, etc. You're getting comfortable with researching on your own by now, right?

What if you find limitations like pain or fear? Remember, they can be completely released — but only when the one with the problem wishes to change. Don't allow your satisfaction in life to depend upon somebody else's choices.

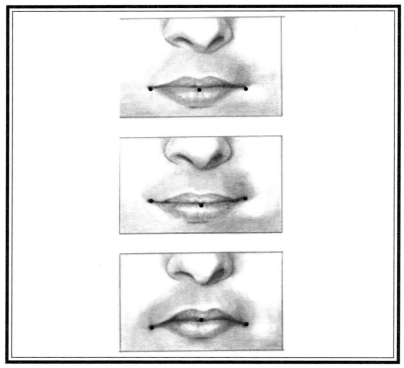

Illustration 19. QUIZ ANSWERS

Meike made this lip quiz extra-easy for you. Each mouth in this collection ends with a sizeable, very distinct, Pain Line (something I describe as "line without lip" on Page 214).

It's easier to follow the angle of a *line* than to find the angle in a three-dimensional *shape,* which most lips have. So let me teach you my "Connect the Dots" method to find angles on a face.

Put a dot at each mouth *edge* plus one in the *center.* Then draw lines to connect each segment. That helps you to read mouth angle on any lips. Usually all the dots and lines are imaginary but I've drawn the dots here to get you started.

Taking it from the top, the answers to our quiz (with or without visual aids) are **even, up,** and **down.**

39. Secretiveness

Hiding a secret or two is no big deal. Major secretiveness is different. It can cover behavior that's devious, coercive, illegal, etc. Under the surface, could your partner be hiding a double life or otherwise be engaged in major deception?

BODY LANGUAGE

During the first few seconds of an encounter, your partner gives a brand new first impression. Pay special attention to the following clues at the eyes and mouth:

Mouth with-holds can signal a problem.

Is the mouth held *tighter* than usual? Lips could look *thinner* than normal, or signs of tension may show in the *corners of the mouth.*

To find out what's going on, start by discussing matters with no big emotional charge. Then ask gently if something is wrong.

Eye changes can expose secretiveness, too.

+ When a partner who usually looks you in the eye suddenly won't, how come?

+ What if you find a guilty expression?

Go on to read deeper. Hey, read deeper even if you find no changes to eyes. The worst secretiveness of all, masking *deliberate dishonesty,* won't show at all nonverbally. Read this reliably only in auras.

Still, another possibility is *secretiveness without dishonesty.* Your partner may simply be a complicated person who needs space.

This could be a non-negotiable requirement for your relationship to work. To identify that kind of secretiveness, read faces.

FACE READING

Emotional patterns of secretiveness shows clearly in face data. But they are highly personal. I recommend that you read the categories in this section only with important relationships in your personal life.

Mouth puckers are tiny dimples at the corners of the mouth. They symbolize a sad kind of secretiveness— fear of asking for what you need and want. (The best example in this book shows on Page 29 with the young man's mouth pucker on the left side only.)

Mouth puckers are caused by a certain kind of discouragement. If you have them now, some time in the past you dared to ask for favors. Unfortunately, you asked the wrong person. Not only weren't you given what was requested. You were mocked for asking.

Even in a loving relationship, asking can make a person feel a bit vulnerable. But a true partnership should include safety for making requests. This should be considered trust, not weakness.

Whoever in your relationship has the mouth puckers can break the secretiveness habit. Start by asking for something small, like a glass of water. Work your way up to what really matters.

Request that backrub or birthday gift. Only time this request as if you were making a marriage proposal. Don't ask until you're reasonably sure that you'll receive a "Yes."

Speak up then. Love does not mean mind reading.

What if your partner's mouth shows **Pain Lines?** This is another little-known sign of secretiveness.

Physically, here's what you see with Pain Lines. When the mouth is in repose, past the lip corners, there's a horizontal line, a kind of "line without lip." You can see two examples in a row on Page 210. Skip the first illustration and find Pain Lines on the two others.

Babies don't have Pain Lines. They develop. Usually the cause is that someone who matters to you has repeatedly stifled your self-expression.

+ Help a partner to heal this pattern by encouraging conversation; then show genuine interest.
+ If you're the one with the Pain Lines, explain about the problem and ask for help with working through it.
  Even if the lines don't disappear, your stored pain can go. With that, you'll release a vicious cycle of secretiveness that leads to feeling more unloved than ever.

Some ears show a **hidden compartment,** formed by cartilage between the inner and outer circles. (See this illustrated on the first ear, Page 192.)

This trait corresponds to a lifelong, unconscious, need for secrecy. What isn't expressed directly may be played out (literally) in music or other creative arts. Respect such a need if you find it in your partner… or yourself.

Finally, **deep-set eyes** signify another form of secretiveness. A profile view makes the data easier to see. But you can see eye set from the front, too, provided that you emphasize the three-dimensional aspect. Some eyes are tucked *inward* beneath the brow bone whereas, with average set, eyes simply lie below the eyebrows.

A deep set means that the eyes are recessed to some degree. For example, see Page 114. In the top right illustration, that right eye is deep set.

Now that you can see it, what's the meaning? A partner with deep-set eyes may be reluctant to discuss problems aloud, yet you can feel the silent judging. Should this happen, encourage candid communication. (Don't complain about the judging aspect, because that's a conversation killer.)

What if you're the one with the deep-set eyes? First, appreciate how your gift for secretiveness helps you to be diplomatic. Second, as they say in the subways of London, "Mind the gap."

If you hide judgments too well, they will harden into contempt, after which you'll never respect your partner again. So take the precaution of expressing complaints while they're reasonably fresh. Be tactful and don't feel that you must deliver the full rant. But do give your partner a clue.

AURAS

Secretiveness isn't always about personal pain. It can signal danger. And the worst kind shows no warning signals with expression. To protect yourself, pay attention at the level of deepest truth, the human energy field.

First, investigate patterns of **verbal secretiveness.** You don't have to be Catholic to know that sins of omission can be just as bad as sins of commission. Begin with your usual Preparation Process: Pay attention to your inner awareness, then Get Big and set an intention to learn about openness vs. secretiveness. (For more details, see Page 25.)

Then plug-in at your partner's Disclosure databank at the Communication Chakra and ask, "How open is his/her communication?"

Secretiveness, if present, could show as holes, disconnects, a sense that the real person has checked out. Sometimes secretiveness freezes just one side of the throat chakra. Problems on the left side relate to relationships, while the right side (as usual) is about work. Major secretiveness at either side could turn your life into hell, so beware.

You might also find it appropriate to check for **spiritual secretiveness.** Your partner may hide a personal agenda about converting you to a different path. Plug-in at the Allowing databank at the Spiritual Chakra and ask, "How does he/she relate to *my* spiritual life?"

To test any negative findings, initiate a conversation, e.g. "Do you believe that one person could know what's best for someone else's spiritual life?"

Hear what your partner says. Read body language as well as any change to his/her aura. Better to bring any unpleasant secret into the open. Hopefully, instead, you'll soon draw a sigh of relief.

40. Self-Disclosure

When does a personal conversation turn too personal? That's a boundary you can learn to recognize — in your partner as well as yourself. Don't expect to find one universal right way to define personal boundaries. But you can find a perfect balance for every relationship in your life now.

BODY LANGUAGE

Alas, body language mostly helps you learn when you have made **mistakes** about self-disclosure. It could seem perfectly fine to share that cute story about your psychopathic uncle or your biggest orgasm, but then...

Kablooey! Too late to retract the words, you know you have said too much because your partner does crossing behavior with legs or arms. (See Page 203.) Or, at the face, any of these signs means that you just blew it:

+ Eyes narrow.
+ The forehead crinkles or wrinkles. Whether those lines are horizontal or vertical, they signal bad news for you.
+ Eyebrows raise. Even worse, you may see the dreaded lifting of the left brow only.
+ Lips thin ominously.
+ Cheek contours change. A stifled grimace shows that your partner has manners (but you have still lost points).
+ The whole face takes on a wooden expression.
+ A throat clears or there's a muffled gasp.
+ Saddest of all, you catch that heinous micro-expression, an upwards eye roll.

What can you do now for damage control? Quick, change the subject. Apologize. Make a joke.

This partner may give you another chance. If so, avoid goofing again. Be proactive and read patterns of self-disclosure in faces and auras.

FACE READING

Self-disclosure tendencies are amazingly easy to read, provided that you let go of one really stooooopid social stereotype. **Lipfulness,** how full or thin lips are, is not about sexiness. Instead, lipfulness reveals comfort with self-disclosure.

Start reading lipfulness by comparing **lip proportions.** Which is fuller, the upper lip or the lower lip? (All three options are illustrated on the facing page.)

+ Most mouths show a *slightly fuller* lower lip. For self-disclosure, that's no biggie. Go on to read overall lipfulness.
+ With an *extra-full lower* lip, the mouth owner dislikes discussing personal matters — yours or anyone else's. Keep this partner content by discussing facts, not feelings.
+ How about someone with an *extra-full upper* lip in proportion to the lower lip? This partner adores discussing the personal side of life. But personal about who, the self or others? Immediately....

Check out **overall lipfulness** by comparing the mouth to other features, e.g., nose tip size, eye height, cheek width. Do lips seem full, thin or moderate?

+ If your partner has *moderate lipfulness,* self-disclosure won't be a big issue. (For illustration, see our top drawing, opposite.)
+ However, very *full lipfulness* means that your partner may often need to discuss personal matters. To this person, self-disclosure makes a conversation authentic. (For illustration, see our bottom drawing, opposite.)
+ Ironically, someone with very thin lipfulness has a different reaction: To this person, self-disclosure makes a conversa-

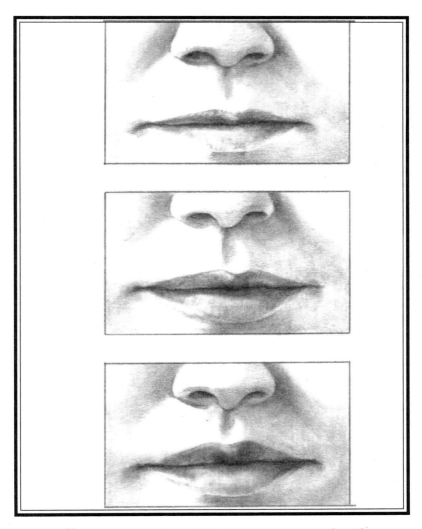

Illustration 20. LIP PROPORTIONS

Taking it from the top, our illustrations show:
+ A slightly fuller lower lip
+ An extra-full lower lip
+ An extra-full upper lip

tion... embarrassing. (For illustration, see Page 89, bottom drawing.)

Gee, could there be a little problem if your partner's lipfulness is the opposite of yours? In work relationships, match your comfort level to that of your boss. For a romantic relationship, I recommend this:

If your lips are way fuller than your partner's, curb your tongue. Find other friends to share the juicy stuff.

But if your lips are way thinner, find a polite way to explain that, for you, self-disclosure, though sweet, must be dispensed in small portions, like slices of a very rich cake.

Either way, see if you and your lover can develop a nonverbal signal that means, "Spare me." Discreet signals, like touching a fingertip to your cheek, will work better than less subtle signals... like smooshing some rich cake into your lover's big mouth.

AURAS

Does your partner's aura contain strong needs or STUFF related to self-disclosure? Either would over-ride anything else that shows in faces or body language. So read away at that innermost level, beginning with your usual Preparation Process. (See page 25.)

Set an intention to learn about self-disclosure. Then plug-in at the Intimacy databank in the Emotional Chakra. Ask, "What kind of conversation would he/she find hard to hear?"

Then plug-in at the databank for Self-Disclosure in Love Relationships in the Communication Chakra. Ask, "What kind of conversation would he/she find hard to hear?"

The answer(s) may surprise you. And educate you.

With practice, you can tell the difference between natural, comfortable personal boundaries versus distortions caused by fear or pain.

That's especially important to distinguish in your own aura, because guess whose job it is to clean that up?

41. Sense of Humor

The funny thing about a sense of humor is how everybody claims to have one. At least everybody can *encourage* the use of that alleged sense of humor. (See the end of this chapter.)

Let's admit it. Some folks have such an undeveloped sense of humor they're more likely to throw you a 90-ton snowball than toss out a spontaneous laugh.

Unless you're a professional comedian, humor won't be the deal breaker in your career. For your personal life, however, things could be different. What if it's important to you that your partner's sense of humor be compatible?

You could whip out a joke book on your first date, read at random, and find out what happens. Alas, there may be no second date.

So try our more subtle approach. Behind the scenes, research humor about *all* the people who matter to you. It could prove seriously useful.

BODY LANGUAGE

When your partner laughs, listen to the **sound quality**. Is it forced, tinny, hollow, or way too hearty? Someone who only pretends to laugh won't fill your life with merriment.

Ears can tell you if laughter is merely polite. Or could it be fully flirtatious but otherwise empty. Often heard on dates are giggles with a subtext. "Aren't I cute? Touch me."

Effective though that may be as a mating signal, never confuse it with having a sense of humor.

Context can also help you interpret this vital nonverbal aspect. Who's being laughed at here? Does the joke involve smooshing somebody's feelings? When an *idea* is the source of humor, that's a different sport from *criticizing* somebody's weight or clothing. When a group is singled out for ridicule, it had better be a group that you despise, too.

Frankly, laughter can signal either **flexibility or rigidity.** Context + sound + expression are all part of the equation.

If you're more visual than auditory, look for *physical flexibility* in your partner's laughter. Like sex, laughter can be mostly in the head. When your partner's laughter becomes a full-bodied experience, that augurs well for having plenty of fun to share through the years.

Next comes sheer **volume** of laughter loudness. Compare that with your partner's speaking voice. Do you hear a restrained giggle or a bring-down-the-house guffaw?

Hushed volume may reveal timidity about giving in to humor, whereas roars of hilarity hint that a great deal of emotion has been processed, in which case consider yourself warned. This person probably deals with lots of emotion at other times, too. How do you feel about having such a zestful companion?

Raucousness could either add years to your life or cause you to die a little, inside, every day. Don't sentence yourself to a relationship where you're laughing on the outside, cringing on the inside.

Finally, watch **facial expression** during laughter. Does your partner's face light up? Excellent. If tears stream out of eyes, even better. What's not so hot having eyes scowl or the whole face turn twisted. Along with that kind of laugh, if you listen perceptively, you'll hear the sound of cruelty.

When you choose a partner whose laughter is compatible with yours, you're well on the way to a relationship that's solid... and maybe even entertaining.

FACE READING

Mouth length and lipfulness combine in fascinating ways to reveal a person's sense of humor. The biggest laughers combine *long* *mouths with full lips.* Nothing is too goofy for them. They'll laugh at slapstick, satire, even practical jokes.

Our best illustration in this book is Page 136, bottom. But the mouth in the drawing is barely long enough and full enough to count as long + full. To find better examples, watch TV. Performers are most likely to have this lip combo; usually it's rare.

Short mouths with full lips don't generally specialize in entertaining the whole room. Private jokes come easier. (For an illustration, see Page 219, bottom.)

Thinner lips suggest someone who finds wit and sarcasm more appealing than physical comedy. Folks with *long, thin lips* are apt to excel as joke tellers, while those with *short, thin lips* make a better audience. (For the former, see Page 56, top left. For the latter, turn to Page 89, left.)

Lips with *moderate length and lipfulness* indicate versatility with humor. Telling jokes may be a strength, but humor can also show in writing, photography or other forms of communication. (See a sample of this common lip configuration at Page 14, middle drawing.)

And for every **cheek dimple** you find, be it peek a boo, permanent or powerline, expect 25% more laughter.

AURAS

Jokes don't tell themselves, and similarly, you need to ask the appropriate question to get the info. you need reading auras. Begin with your usual Preparation Process. See Page 25.

Set an intention to open up your heart. Then plug-in at the Sense of Humor databank at the Communication Chakra. Ask, "What makes him/her laugh?"

On rare occasions, you'll find a soul-level gift for comedy. This is so refreshing to read that I urge you to linger if you find it. Wallow in that throat chakra. Feel the sparkle bubbles!

Laugh More

The more ex-partners you have, the harder it can be to pick yourself up, dust yourself off, and laugh yourself back to normal.

Small annoyances can be irksome. Wish you could laugh them off but you just can't? Well, have I got a technique for you! Try this technique to switch on your sense of humor on demand.

Say out loud, "Ha ha, ho ho, he he." Repeat these sounds until you start to laugh out loud.

Does the "Ha ha" sound fake? No problem. If you're in a really stinky mood, you can purposely make it sound sarcastic, angry, or otherwise nasty.

Eventually the rage will peel off and you'll be left laughing.

Don't just take my word for it. Open up your mouth and say it out loud: "Ha ha, ho ho, he he. Ha ha, ho ho, he he. Ha ha, ho ho, he he. Ha ha, ho ho, he he."

Caution: Be careful not to substitute **inadequate** *words like "Tee hee." Unless you really make that sound when you laugh, "Tee hee" will not switch on your giggle reflex. "Tee hee" is a dud. Try it.*

But if your soul cries out for variety, you might get away with using Jackie Gleason's phrase. Ever see "The Honeymooners" on TV? When really stressed out, Gleason's character used to bellow, "Har, har, hardee har har."

His goal was to make the audience laugh, not his own character, so he only said it once. Once isn't enough to activate your own laughter mechanism, not unless you're pretty far gone.

To use Gleason's **laughter sutra** *as an actual technique, you've got to repeat the words several times. (How many is several? Be careful not to count, unless you find numbers hysterically funny.) Soon, as if by magic, you'll revert to "Ha ha, ho ho, he he." And you just might be laughing.*

42. Sensitivity

Quick, what's your gut reaction to the question, "Are you sensitive?"

To paraphrase psychologist Elaine Aron's landmark book, *Highly Sensitive Persons,* here's the response you would get from giving five people a sensitivity questionnaire:

+ One says, "Sensitive? Am I ever!"
+ One says, "Sensitive? Come to think of it, yes."
+ One looks puzzled. "Sensitivity isn't a big issue for me, either way."
+ Two say something like, "What, that pathetic and disgusting weakness? No way."

Sensitivity is a kind of inner wiring of the nervous system, not something a person can change. Yet sensitivity is widely disrespected by those who don't have it, and "they" are the majority of human beings.

If *less sensitive* than your partner, you get to be "the rock of stability" in the relationship, able to protect and support. You can comfort him/her though your physical presence. This will win you relationship points, provided you also show respect for that sensitivity.

What if you are the *more sensitive* one? You'll have valuable insights to share with your partner about business. For a love relationship, you'll bring perceptiveness about behavior from family members and friends.

Plus, your more refined perception can help to upgrade your mate's quality of life, everything from buying furniture to gauging how loud to turn on the TV. (Incidentally, you're probably the one who should do the cooking.)

How can you lose points? By coming across as a whiner.

Besides your overall physiological sensitivity, you and your partner each have *sensitivity specialties,* like the need for fresh air or music sung in tune. Learn more about them by reading deeper.

BODY LANGUAGE

How fast can the less sensitive partner make the other one cringe? Quicker than you might think. Reading deeper, you may find problems related to what I call **sensitivity trespass**, where one partner hurts the other's feelings.

Even if this happens unintentionally, damage is done. Yet you can do damage control, provided that you notice the problem. How can you become sensitive to your lack of sensitivity? Read microexpressions. Why micro? You're dealing with an unconscious, instinctive response, not a conscious social gesture.

Looking away can be response to sensitivity trespass. Eyes dart downward or blink extra fast as the sufferer attempts avoidance.

Then there's *sound*. A quick, quiet sigh (more a thickening of breath than a voiced, dramatic exhale) signals the need for TLC.

Quick *lip movements* can reveal a problem with sensitivity trespass. The following list shows a variety of not-quite conscious expressions, complete with translations:

+ Lips draw inward, making the mouth appear narrower. "Should I tell you I'm upset? No, I'll suffer in silence."
+ A pout is quickly made, then quickly retracted. "Do I dare speak up for what I need? No. What's the use?"
+ Lips are bitten just slightly, on the inside edge. "Ooh, I don't like what's going on. Still, I'd better not speak up."
+ Very faint pressure is used to suck in the lips. "Here we go again. I hate this. Of course, it won't help to say so."

Are these translations guaranteed accurate? No, life isn't that simple. But you can find out. Ask, "Is something bothering you?" Listen sympathetically and you will set the stage for future closeness.

What happens if you ignore these micro-expressions? Subtlety will give way to exaggeration. For instance, weeks later, you'll hear a "sigh" that could blow out a candle.

Are you the one who sighs? Stop hinting and speak your mind. Is this your partner or your prison guard?

FACE READING

To read physiological sensitivity read **skin texture.** Twice. Read it on the main part of the face. Then read it on ears. The contrast may astonish you.

Start with **facial** skin texture. Faces can be either thin-skinned, thick-skinned, or moderately thick-skinned.

To help you develop your eye, think of skin like frosting on a cake. Is the cake barely covered, like a lightly glazed donut or, at the other extreme, more like cake slathered with frosting?

Compare several faces and soon you'll be able to read this category. Then read it on yourself and your partner.

Facial skin texture relates to *social sensitivity,* how your personality comes across when you're in a crowd.

Thin skin suggests that you're sensitive and it shows, even to casual observers. At best, you'll be treated extra considerately. At worst, you'll be resented or ridiculed.

Thick skin indicates a personality that seems well adjusted, definitely an advantage for fitting in. Folks with similar skin texture will consider you psychologically stable, a good sport, fun to be with. What's your potential challenge? You risk striking sensitives as an inconsiderate oaf. Oops!

Moderately thick skin suggest no worries about social sensitivity. Your challenge is lack of tolerance for the rest of humanity. Why should other people have problems with seeming either overly sensitive or insensitive? (Because they're not you, that's why!)

Next, for contrast, read **ear texture.** The texture of skin here has no relationship to what you've seen about skin on the face as a whole.

Silky ear texture means the ear has been put together with a minimum of skin, so it may seem practically transparent.

Fleshy ear texture means that the entire outer ear (not just the lobe) appears thick and solid.

Moderately fleshy ear texture falls between the two extremes.

Ear texture equates to *mind-body-spirit sensitivity*, how a person has been wired since birth to respond to life. Ears reveal a secret, more private version of social sensitivity, and it may be a total contrast to what shows in a crowd.

• Silky ear texture indicates the greatest innate sensitivity.

• Fleshy ear texture accompanies a rugged nervous system.

• Moderate fleshiness goes with a flexible nervous system.

Whatever you have, accept it. That's the first lesson for successfully handling sensitivity issues in any relationship.

Then give your partner acceptance as well. Stop expecting him/her to be "just like me." Respect can make any combo work.

AURAS

Even if you're not especially sensitive, you can be great at aura reading. You can be a desirable partner in every way. So you have nothing to lose by researching this category.

Begin with your usual Preparation Process. (See Page 25.) Set an intention to learn about your partner's sensitivity. Choose any chakra and databank you like. After you plug-in ask, "What shows here in terms of sensitivity?"

Whatever the databank, you may find patterns of literalness or abstraction; thick, dense energy or fine, light energy. Reading many databanks, an overall pattern may show: living at a high or low vibration, a heavier or lower texture, color that is clearer or muddier.

Just as God is in the details, exceptions to this pattern are highly significant. If, regarding sensitivity, one databank seems markedly different from the rest, plug-in and ask, "What does it mean that this databank seems so different from the rest?"

The answer could involve healing in progress, blockage, recovery from trauma or, simply, higher standards for the aspect of life connected to that databank. Open your heart — something else everyone can do regardless of innate sensitivity.

The Silver Rule

When you and your partner disagree over everyday choices, who should rule? At work, it's the boss. Otherwise, it's the one whose needs are more refined. He/she will suffer more if disregarded.

Sure, the less sensitive partner may hate to compromise, but that has more to do with wanting to get your way than being in physical or psychological pain. In return, the more sensitive partner should give something in return. Hence this Silver Rule:

Honor the needs of the more sensitive person in the relationship. If you are the one receiving the kindness, find a way to return the favor every time.

How would this Silver Rule work in practice?

COMFORT

More Sensitive Partner: You hate to sleep on polyester sheets. Like the heroine of the fairytale "Princess and the Pea," you have your reasons. Explain that you need to sleep on pure cotton.
More Rugged Partner: Buy the more expensive sheets, but... give More Sensitive the job of making your bed.

CLEANLINESS

More Sensitive Partner: Compared to your partner, you have a higher standard for cleanliness around the home.
More Rugged Partner: You agree to put things away in shared spaces, but... More Sensitive does the cleaning (or pays for a maid).

CLUTTER

More Sensitive Partner: Every relationship has a saver and a tosser. As the saver, it upsets you enormously to have things thrown away.
More Rugged Partner: You let your mate keep the stuff, but... together you decide how much room in your home is available for stuff. Then More Sensitive must honor that agreement.

43. Sensuousness

Sensuousness is the ultimate form of multi-tasking. Enjoying the pleasures of your senses… hey, you can sneak that in anywhere, any time, no matter what else you are doing.

Increase your sensuousness by reading it: in strangers, while you watch TV, and definitely in any partner who matters to you.

BODY LANGUAGE

Hand behavior could be more important to your relationship than being handsome. Observe how your partner moves hands while talking. Are they flexible, stiff, forceful, sensitive, creative, responsive? (Yes, hands can definitely be considered phallic symbols.)

A partner who prizes sensuousness will show it in **grooming**, especially of hands.

They're vital sensual tools So it's revealing to see if they're either showcased or neglected. How much care has gone into the nails? Have those hands been kept clean? Wallowing in dirt can be sensuous, too. Be honest about what appeals to you.

Touch quality, from those very same hands, is another tip-off to sensuousness. How does your partner handle objects? Watch him/ her pick up car keys or hold a glass of water.

Do sparks fly when your partner's fingers make contact with your body? Be it a handshake, a shoulder pat, or a caress of your cheek, some hands shine like spotlights for *physical intelligence*.

Other kinds of sensuousness show that a person is *awake intuitively*. Does your partner's hand seem to read your emotions, your energy, your sexual interest, how you feel physically?

Especially if you are a skilled empath, you can tell another empath by touch. Are you, the relationship reader, being read?

Illustration 21. Sensory Preference

Use a person's nose as your point of reference in comparing the proportions of a person's eyes and ears.

+ Top: **Eye** length is shorter than nose *tip*.
+ Bottom: **Ear** is longer than nose *length* (bridge-to-tip).

For him, ears are proportionally larger than eyes. How about you?

FACE READING

The proportion of features will tell you if someone is strongly drawn to auditory or visual triggers for sensuousness. Use your partner's nose as your point of reference.

Compared to his/her *length of the nose,* are the ears long or short? *Long ears* relate to awareness of sound. Playing music or hearing a brook babble, a long-eared partner finds sound stimulating. By contrast, *short ears* suggest that sound is unlikely to serve as a major trigger for sensuousness.

Now use the *size of your partner's nose tip* as a reference point for eye proportions. Bigger or smaller? *Big eyes* relate to visual awareness as an indispensible part of sensuousness. With *small eyes,* visuals don't turn into physicals, at least not often. Sensory strengths could be kinesthetic, auditory, empathic, or intuitive, just not visual.

Next, consider the **relative size of features** overall. Do eyes, ears, nose, and mouth dominate the face, or do they seem smaller than areas like the forehead, cheeks and chin?

Larger features overall correspond to an earthier sensuality.

Smaller features suggest that thinking matters as much as physicality, and perception overall may be relatively detached. This person could care more about thinking, emotions, or spirituality, with less investment in physical pleasure for its own sake.

Finally, read lips to discover more about sensuousness. Specifically, examine your partner's **point of refinement.** This tiny mouth area is the facial junction between sensuousness and sexiness. Aim your gaze right at the center of the mouth, between the lips. Do you see a triangle of flesh, adding an extra bit of oomph when making contact with the lower lip?

+ The *more definition* you see at the point of refinement, the more automatically sensuousness turns into sexiness.
+ With *less definition,* there's an equal and opposite advantage. Your partner enjoys sensuousness without feeling the

need to do The Deed. That can mean hours per day of shared pleasure that, like an exquisite wine, will only intensify through the years.

AURAS

Even a happy, well adjusted person may underuse the potential for sensuousness. Once you actively read auras, you'll find it fascinating how each person has distinctive pleasure styles that express nothing less than the **soul.**

I define "soul" as the way your unique qualities as an individual are expressed in your human life. For example, think *soul food*, a form of sensuousness that appeals to taste. Or how about *soul music*, sensual pleasure via hearing? Either one makes you feel more fully alive. Sensuousness is a natural expression of the soul.

My research, reading auras, suggests that only about 1 in 300 people today enjoy their human lives very much. Why not?

Lives can emphasize many things other than the soul, such as duty, sex, competition, or spiritual interests. Many alleged "virtues," such as sacrifice, are like poison to the soul. Placing family needs above your own happiness can be carried too far, as can programming you may have received that (supposedly) your main job in a relationship is to anticipate the other person's needs.

But anyone can claim soulfulness by spending an hour a day on activities that you really enjoy. This makes the corresponding part of your aura big and perky.

Begin research with your usual Preparation Process. (See Page 25.) Set an intention to learn what thrills your soul. Plug-in to the Soul Expression databank at your Soul Chakra and preview what it would be like to live juicy. Ask "What would happen to me if I took more time every day to enjoy my sensuality?"

Then, if you're very bold, follow up by asking, "What activities that I'm not doing now… would thrill my soul?"

44. Sex Drive

There you are, standing in the car lot of love. Whether you're choosing a new model or trading up from an old one, wouldn't it be great to go for a test drive before you buy?

That's what deeper perception is for. Preview the sexual performance of a new love vehicle—or re-evaluate what you're driving now.

Read yourself, too, while you're at it. If you love to drive fast, how compatible will you be with a car that barely makes it out of first gear? Yet a model with super-high sex drive may be too "expensive" for you energetically, throwing your wheels out of alignment. Research your love interest now to learn about compatibility.

BODY LANGUAGE

Here's where body language offers you enormous amounts of information. I'll give you nine (count 'em, 9!!!!!!!!!!) different things to watch for. Body language is the best way to read this category. There is so much research you can do without anyone else suspecting.

First, consider **physical ease**, which means your partner's degree of relaxation when doing ordinary things. What is his/her tempo for moving, talking, walking, even picking up the phone? Dawdling may be bad for time management but it's great for sex drive.

Think about it. After sex, people relax. In fact, it may be the only time when some people relax (other than sleep). Highly sexed people remember how to shift into the slow, full timing of physical pleasure.

Now here's the exception that proves the rule. If the person you're watching seems hyper, are there micro-expressions about relaxing? Many a high-powered achiever shows super-quick moments of physical ease, or desire. Go straight to aura reading to find out more. Busy people who love contrast can be the hottest lovers of all.

Second, **contagious ease** means that your partner's degree of physical ease increases in your presence. If your date seems more relaxed after the two of you have spent some time together, that's a good sign of compatible sex drive. On the other hand....

Third, factor in **sexual tension.** Symptoms include:

+ Blushing, flushing or otherwise feeling hot
+ Intensity in your voices, the pace of your words
+ A sense that the very air around you is highly charged
+ Intensified sexual daydreams while you're together

Of course, the ultimate symptom of sexual tension is difficulty keeping your hands off each other. By then, you're no longer just reading body language.

Fourth, a man's **sexual alertness** is worth noting. Male partners have a cute way of showing it, which you may politely gauge with a quick peek.

Fifth, for women, read **breast presentation.** Does posture cause those bumpers to stick out or slump over? In addition to walking proud, a woman with strong sex drive will move her torso as if fully loaded. Sometimes she will even position her arms protectively. Rather than emphasizing size, a discerning partner will notice if the woman moves as though she's glad she has breasts.

Sixth, you can read sex drive from gestures. You can feel if your partner moves with **sexual self-consciousness.** There's a kind of subtext to gestures, as if to say, "The way you're watching me right now, hey, this could be a kind of preview."

If you're still not sure what I mean by sexual self-consciousness, TV can be a great teaching tool. Watch any show where flirting or seduction are involved. Some shows turn up the intensity of sexual self-consciousness, others don't. In life, an adult directs his/her performance in every scene, either remembering to include sex or not.

Seventh, read your date's **walk** to learn about sex drive. Begin with the category of *horizontal vs. vertical.* Experienced partners have lost the up-and-down walk known as "the virgin bounce." Hot hetero women swivel their hips a lot (and some gay men do a more restrained version). By contrast, straight men and some gay men and lesbians do the opposite, walking with hips quite steady.

Eight, score extra points for sex drive when the walk suggests **pelvic self-consciousness.** Yes, some guys walk as if well aware that they carry the family jewels, just as certain women nonverbally flaunt their booty.

Ninth, to complete your sex drive survey, combine all that you've read so far with overall **physical coordination**

Is movement fluid, stiff, or jerky? A graceful, full-bodied walk signals physical ability. But maybe that's just because he/she did sports in high school.

The combination of coordination with sexual self-consciousness is what tells you that, sexually, you're about to hook up with a Lexus.

FACE READING

What a fascinating mystery, how lips meet—and not for just kissing, either. Pay attention to the joining of upper and lower lips on your partner's mouth. You'll be rewarded with superior insight into sex drive.

Lip compression is one of those things about the face you've had the opportunity to see your whole life. But have you ever paid attention? When reading sex drive, you can gauge the amount of pressure between your partner's lips.

A *soft line* means that upper and lower lips meet with the gentlest of pressures, something you can spot by the line itself (which may include tiny gaps). Also, you might notice the shape of the lips right where they meet. Softness equals voluptuousness.

Even more extreme is a *parted line*. Assuming that your partner isn't a perpetual mouth breather, a mouth that opens slightly in your presence shows a super-intense sex drive.

A *hard line* looks as though the upper and lower lips have been squished together, revealing a habitual lack of sensuousness.

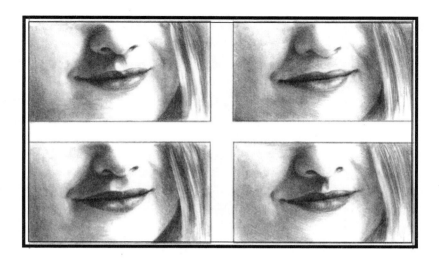

Illustration 22. PHILTRUM GALLERY

The philtrum, or overlip, links nose and mouth. Here we're looking at width. Reading from left to right, top to bottom:
+ Even — and wide— philtrum
+ No philtrum width (Not every face shows a well-defined philtrum. Read more about this on Page 66.)
+ Extra-wide, and widening, philtrum
+ Narrow philtrum

Normally, that mouth is slammed shut. Admittedly, when your partner does choose to be sensuous, the quality may be superb.

Where Sex Shows Most on a Face

Allow me to introduce you to the **philtrum.** (You could also call it "the overlip.") Look at the twin ridges extending from nose bottom to upper lip. In later chapters, we'll research several important categories to be found in this part of the face. Here, let's focus on one:

philtrum width. The philtrum is twin ridges between nose and mouth. **Philtrum width** is the horizontal distance between those twin ridges. Compare the width at the top to the width at the bottom. Is it *wider, narrower* or *even*?

A philtrum that *widens* symbolizes increasing sex drive. When a philtrum *narrows*, that suggests moving forward on the initial momentum, with other interests (like emotional bonding) becoming as important as the physical act itself. An *even* philtrum corresponds to consistent interest in sex.

Alas, problems with physical or psychological health can temporarily lessen sex drive, no matter how much lustiness shows in a philtrum. Scope out problems by reading auras.

AURAS

Sex drive can change because of what your lover is going through now, plus past fears or pain. It may sound cold-hearted to snoop in advance of becoming involved. But, honestly, what's more frustrating than to start making love, then have everything fizzle?

To research, do your usual Preparation Process. (See Page 25.) Set an intention to learn dispassionately. Then plug-in at the Libido databank in the Sexual Chakra and ask, "How big is his/her sex drive?" To follow up, ask, "Does any sexual problem show up?"

You can also research related databanks at this same chakra. For the Creative Flow databank, plug-in again and ask, "What's happening with his/her creativity?"

Also inquire at the Inner Child databank, "How spontaneously does he/she express desire?"

Remember, problems can always be healed if the person commits to healing it. Back in the days of Freud, you'd have to lie on the healer's couch for an awfully long time. Healing can be far quicker today. If your partner is willing, today's holistic healing modalities can work miracles.

Preview a Lover Sexually

It's a funny thing about sex; I've noticed that some people become very shy about reading it in auras. Could you have a double standard?

Did you get all timid and squirmy about reading the nine types of body language in this chapter? Well then, don't suddenly think it's weird to read auras.

As long as you keep what you learn to yourself, you have every right to preview a new date sexually. And, if you have a long-term lover, of course it's okay to do this kind of research.

Ethically, you must always do what seems right to you. Personally, I don't believe that I need to ask permission to read **anything** *about anyone's aura.*

Telling *what you find is different. There, privacy must be respected, unless the person has chosen to be a celebrity. Even then, for pity's sake, don't put the results of aura research about sex on your blog.*

45. Sexual Adventurousness

You can be hot as all get-out yet prefer your love-making on the predictable side. Wouldn't it be nice to know whether you and your date wants what... before you jump into bed, hammock or igloo?

Asking could be embarrassing. But detective work about adventurousness can become your discreet little secret.

BODY LANGUAGE

Eating reveals so much about sex, it's amazing that couples can have dinner dates without blushing. To read sexual adventurousness, choose from the following nonverbal menu.

When the two of you are at a restaurant, note body language while **ordering** the food. How does your partner express what he/she wants? Ordering can be done *decisively* or *with waffles* (and I'm not talking about the breakfast kind). Does your lover expect you to take the lead? If ordering is done for you, is it done with charming sophistication or just plain pushy?

Sometimes a partner will *complicate* ordering, requesting substitutions, demanding a special degree of rareness, or asking interminable questions about what is to be provided.

Easy to please? Hardly. Sexual travels with a fussy companion will most likely leave you feeling bad about yourself.

Read **food preferences** to predict the nature of your sexual liaisons. A meat-and-potatoes gal may not yearn for the same kind of thrills as a guy who buys Thai.

Observe **eating priorities** to fine-tune the sexual message. Does he/she sample each item in sequence or methodically start with the protein, finish it all, go on to the first vegetable, etc.? Your lover's approach will be a deal breaker only if you find it annoying.

Condiment behavior is also sexually revealing. Your date's enjoyment of food presages how you'll be treated when you're the main dish. Who salts the food before tasting? Do puddles of ketchup bother you?

Spices, salsas and chutneys, used discretely, show a discerning flair for adventurousness. But someone who slathers the chili with hot sauce may be more interested in novelty than seasoning. Interpret that as a big list of partners but teensy versatility.

Table manners can parallel sex etiquette. Does your date put on a show the first time you eat and greet, using extra-enticing, company-style table manners? Or is what you see at the first meal what you'll get for the rest of your lives together?

A partner who slaps elbows on the table and shovels food from plate to mouth may be sexually adventurous, but no change of positions will alter the overall pattern of crudeness.

Sharing counts, too. Will your sexual adventures be shared or turn out more like parallel play? To anticipate the difference, watch how your partner alternates paying attention to the food with paying attention to *you*.

First Base and Beyond

Research into body language worldwide shows that there really is something to the expression "getting to first base." Like baseball, sex has a sequence for scoring. But did you know that, even before that first kiss, body language takes you around a predictable circuit?

Benefit from your partner's built-in sequence for sex and take it one step at a time. No matter how adventurous both of you are, don't experiment with this sequence until your second time together.

Otherwise, your attentions may result in behavior like this: Frowns, angry blushing, contracting eye pupils, avoiding your eyes, nervous laughter, the sound of a slap, a hasty exit. Don't continue your advances or you'll be called a "Masher" or worse. But if you see signs like the following, be encouraged, be very encouraged.

FIRST BASE. The Look of Love

+ Unconscious *self-touching* is done, like your partner stroking his/her own arm.
+ Objects are played with like sexual *symbols,* consciously or not (e.g. Slowly eating a long pretzel, fingering the loops of a round pretzel).
+ The first testing, *teasing touch* "spontaneously" happens (e.g., His/her leg "accidentally" brushes against yours).
+ Playfully, the two of you exchange *experimental touches* (e.g., You spar with teasing pushes against each other's shoulders).
+ Your partner's *head tilts* towards you.
+ Your partner's breast or *chest tilts* towards you.
+ Your partner's *hips tilt* towards you. When head, chest, and hips all line up, it's like a Las Vegas slot machine coming up all cherries!
+ Your partner's *eyes widen,* increasing their degree of roundness.
+ The whole *face softens,* relaxing.
+ Eyes *brighten.*
+ *Blinking* rate shifts. Either eyes gaze with less blinking than usual or the eyelashes flutter.
+ *Eyebrows* lift.
+ *Mouth position* becomes self-conscious, with subtle (or not so subtle) differences in how lips are held compared to normal.
+ *Posture improves,* presenting your partner at his/her most attractive (e.g., No slouches or slumps).
+ *Facial color* perks up. A becoming blush may appear.

All these changes make your partner look extra attractive. Love light increases at his/her aura, too. Extra energy pours out of the Sexual Chakra. Extra light also radiates from the Emotional Chakra, plus any other chakras where the two of you make an especially strong connection.

SECOND BASE. Moving into the Sexual Zone

+ Proxemics alert: Whatever the usual amount of space between you two, small gestures test your *moving closer.*
+ Your partner leans toward you, and the *leaning is mutual.*
+ Conversation becomes whispered, with his/her *voice* becoming increasingly tender.
+ The *pace of conversation* slows to a crawl.
+ *Gestures,* too, become slower and charged with sexual electricity.

Your auras start to pulsate in synch.

THIRD BASE. Both of You Know What's Coming Next

+ Physically, you draw *closer still,* giving each other exclusive attention.
+ Unconsciously you *mirror* each other's physical position.
+ *Preening* gestures are made, like touching hair.
+ There's a *smile.* It may be a special kind of smile not shown before.
+ Directly or symbolically, your conversation shifts to *"Are you interested?"*
+ *Breathing* shifts, slowing or panting or shirting. (Just kidding about that last one.)
+ Eyes lock.
+ *Lips* lock.

Aurically, you're starting to merge. If either of you typically has protective walls at the level of a chakra—most commonly at the Emotional or Sexual Chakra—that wall may come tumbling down, temporarily at least. Expect a home run.

FACE READING

To appreciate fine points about your lover's sexual adventurousness, let's revisit the category called facial **priority areas,** starting on Page 114.

Review how to measure these three face lengths. Then we can apply the data to sexual adventurousness.

+ Priority **Area I Biggest:** Ideas fascinate your lover. So mind games, fantasy, and wild ideas may spice up lovemaking.

+ Priority **Area II Biggest:** Ambition and ego mean a lot to your lover. Use praise to maximize desire for adventure. You might even motivate this kind of lover by keeping a scorecard of your different locations, different positions.

+ Priority Area **III Biggest:** Sex is never far away from your lover's mind. Add to the sense of adventure by experimenting with clothes, massage oils and fragrances, even sex toys.

+ All Three Priority **Areas Equal:** Your lover is uncommonly versatile, with many interests and a natural ability to keep them in balance.

+ Priority **Area I Smallest:** Discuss ideas during sex only if you wish to be ignored — or watch your partner wilt.

+ Priority **Area II Smallest:** This kind of lover will work harder than most to satisfy you. Give a clear message about the sort of adventure that you desire.

+ Priority **Area III Smallest:** For your partner, sex carries great symbolic importance.

To enhance adventure, find out the main themes in your partner's belief system (e.g., Expressing love, spiritual union). Then introduce variety in terms of that belief system. (e.g., "This book on *tantra* might help us to grow spiritually.")

AURAS

For adventurousness, your lover's Sexual Chakra matters as much as any physical attributes. And size is just one component.

Begin with your usual Preparation Process: Pay attention to your inner awareness, then Get Big and set an intention to explore with Beginner's Mind. (For more details, see Page 25.)

Plug-in at the Sexual Adventurousness databank in the Sexual Chakra. Ask, "How does he/she relate to being sexually adventurous?"

The answer may surprise you. Auras will teach you, again and again, about the uniqueness of each individual. For your own protection, explore these follow-up questions:

+ "Does he/she have an appetite for sexual cruelty?"
+ "Is danger a turn-on?"

The answers could make all the difference between a delightful adventure and a horror story.

46. Sexual Promiscuity

Flattering though it is to have a hotshot lover want you, what can really wreck your enjoyment? The crowd waiting in line....

Promiscuity can be a fun way of life, provided that you're both willing to be honest about it (and both of you use condoms). What doesn't work is sneaking. Do you want to be the last to know about your lover's promiscuity?

Of course, with deeper perception you can do the research. In this Age of AIDS, you'd better. Reading for sexual promiscuity could save your life.

BODY LANGUAGE

As always, body language is an especially good way to learn about sex. Tight, **body-conscious clothes** are revealing in more ways than one. Unless those garments are worn in privacy, your partner is revealing potential promiscuity. The chance of this increases with each of the following nonverbal signs, while in your presence, used toward *other* people:

- Ultra-long *eye contact*
- *Squeezing* lips into a pout
- *Moistening* lips with the tongue
- *Opening* the mouth
- *Licking* the teeth
- Staring hard or *winking*
- Crossing or *uncrossing* legs
- *Stroking* or rearranging the hairstyle
- *Touching* his/her face or body
- Making suggestive use of *props* like cigarettes or food

Another promiscuity indicator is having an acquaintance boldly stare at your intimate areas, or take many furtive, fascinated peeks.

Even if this would-be friend isn't as promiscuous as body language would suggest, he/she is demonstrating a certain lack of finesse. Depending on your own inclinations, unabashed come-ons could heat up your sex life. But don't think there's anything wrong with you sexually if a promiscuous lover's hot flash leaves you cold.

FACE READING

Remember the philtrum, that area between nose and mouth that's about sex appeal? Long-term lasciviousness can cause the entire overlip area to stick out like... a sore thumb. If you prefer exclusive monogamous relationships, beware a **raised philtrum.**

Free will being what it is, no face data guarantees promiscuity. But the owner of such a philtrum will struggle more than others would to stay monogamous, and it won't hurt you to do the occasional reading for fidelity. (See Pages 131-133.)

Another unusual but important characteristic is **philtrum tilt.** Do the twin ridges of the philtrum lean to one side? To see this, compare the philtrum at the top (just below the nose) to the bottom (near the mouth).

If the left side of the face is favored, you're looking at a *left-angled philtrum.* This suggests a strong and constant yearning for sex, beyond all other interests in personal life. And no, all red-blooded men do not have this.

A *right-angled philtrum* warns you that this lover may be tempted to use sex appeal for career enhancement. Actually, you call find two examples of this on Page 237, the two lower pictures.

For perspective on a philtrum that leans toward the right, remember that sex appeal isn't only about doing The Big One. Strong sex appeal makes people wake up, unconsciously feel attracted to the philtrum wearer, listen extra intently to what he/she has to say.

So a right-angled philtrum could be considered a valuable soul-level gift for career success. Promiscuity, by contrast, is a choice.

A **cleft chin** suggests that your partner may wrestle with sexual temptation, while a **dimpled chin** is signals temptation-lite. Here's someone who may be prone to serial monogamy, though not outright promiscuity. To learn about your partner's response when faced with temptation, you could hire a private detective. But reading auras is cheaper.

AURAS

Go straight for the gusto. Begin with your usual Preparation Process (see Page 25) and set the intention to be a bold explorer.

Plug into the Libido databank at the Sexual Chakra. Ask, "What is the size and quality of energy?" Promiscuity creates an especially festive display.

When you have read Sexual Chakras on a variety of people — which, fortunately, does not make *you* promiscuous — you'll become familiar with the following nuances.

Promiscuity brings a sleazy quality, different from sexual addiction or one-time infidelity. (See Pages 48-50 and 131-133.)

Do **pornography** and phone sex count as sexual promiscuity? The model, etc., has an aura. Using him/her for a turn-on will dump that person's vibes into the porno-user's aura. Sound enticing?

How about **masturbation**? Some can be good. Orgasm pulls all the chakras into the equivalent of a washing machine's spin cycle. Unless major guilt is involved, masturbation can cleanse an aura, thus giving new meaning to expressions like "Clean up your act."

But **excessive masturbation** is different. "Excessive" means, *physically,* an amount that causes the person to feel chronically drained. *Psychologically,* it's a compulsion rather than an occasional choice. *Aurically,* energy at the Sexual Chakra becomes way larger than elsewhere in the aura.

Like excessive anything — talking, loving, praying — sexual excess will distort the proportions within an aura.

47. Sexual Stamina

Which type of lover would you rather have, a sprinter or a long-distance runner? Once you decide, read stamina.

BODY LANGUAGE

Here's one instance where body language won't tell you much… short of what that body does with yours while you're in the sack. But before engaging in that kind of research, why not keep your clothes on a tad longer while you read faces and auras?

FACE READING

Philtrum length reveals a lot about sexual stamina. Reading it is simple. Look at the vertical distance between the nose tip and upper lip. Is it long, short or moderate?

On Page 237, a *short* philtrum is pictured on the bottom right. (The philtrum shown at the bottom left is the longest on that page but has only moderate length. You'll know "long" when you see it.)

A *long* philtrum translates into exceptional sexual stamina, both long-term and while you are in the act.

A partner who's well endowed with philtrum length is well adapted to long courtships, since flirting won't use up most of his/her sexual energy. And, of course, sexual stamina adds fun to love making, especially when the partner also has a long fuse.

Don't worry, though, if that fascinating hottie in your life has a short philtrum. This symbolizes a gift for oomphy encounters. And sometimes the shortest ones can be the most memorable. Once he/she becomes involved physically, the philtrum owner gives and receives to the max.

It's intense. Then it's over.

The potential challenge is maintaining long-term interest in a relationship. If you're the one whose philtrum is short, it may help to think of each day as a new relationship, a new chance, rather than a mere continuation of same old, same old.

What if your lover has *moderate philtrum length?* Sexual stamina is flexible. Other things being equal (admittedly, something you never can count on with sex), you can trust that your level of interest will be matched by your lover's.

Okay, your research is off to a good start. Whether a lover's interest tends to last for a long or short time, you're prepared. Now read auras for more spicy details.

AURAS

Guess where you'll start your research? Of course, check out the Sexual Chakra. Begin with your usual Preparation Process: Pay attention to your inner awareness, then Get Big and set an intention to learn about sexual stamina. (For more details, see Page 25.)

Plug-in at the Libido databank. Ask, "How much energy is available for sex?"

Stored-up STUFF can cause impotence or lack of enjoyment, so be sure to follow up by asking, "Is there sexual blockage at this time?"

So far so good? Sex being as complex as it is, however, you'd also be wise to do extra research.

+ Plug-in at the Confidence databank at the Power Chakra and ask, "Are there power issues that affect sex?"
+ At the Emotional Balance databank at the Emotional Chakra, plug-in and ask, "Do any emotional issues affect sex?"
+ Finally, at the Health databank in the Physical Chakra, plug in and ask these two questions, "Do physical issues affect sex?" and "Do any life traumas or disappointments affect sex?"

Sex does start in the head... and the aura. So if you find cause for concern, it may be an opportunity to heal some other aspect of life. Sexual problems, painful though they are, can become motivation to grow. Even people who ordinarily scoff at psychology or metaphysics will pay attention when The Big One is at stake.

Discovering Where Heaven Meets Earth

Celibacy is one way to express spiritual commitment. But if you're reading this part of the book, I have a hunch that celibacy is not your path. Instead you're a householder, someone who evolves spiritually by having little things like a home, a job, personal ambitions, money, and, if you're lucky, a fabulous lover.

Can a householder care about God? Of course, and judging from clients who come to me for sessions of Aura Transformation, more people than you might guess are former priests, nuns, or monks. These recovering celibates are learning how to be humanly happy.

Without having taken an official vow of celibacy, you still may feel ambivalent about sex, worried that it clashes with your spiritual path. I invite you to use deeper percepton to understand your sexual style as part of a glorious spiritual life. I call this "Discovering where heaven meets earth."

All the face reading you've done so far in this book has shown you gifts that you have in life. Your sexual style is just part of that glorious configuration. Round out the picture by reading **philtrum depth.**

To see it, first remember to wear a straight face while doing research. No yawning! No sobbing! It would distort the data.

Looking into the mirror, at a straight angle, observe the ridges that run between nose and mouth, your philtrum. Now, notice the overall depth between those twin ridges. Is it very deep, moderately deep, or shallow? You'll find all three possibilities illustrated on Page 237.

- On the bottom, left picture, the woman's philtrum is very deep.
- The illustration above shows a philtrum with moderate depth.
- Then, in the upper right corner, you'll find a shallow philtrum. (And if you can't really see much philtrum at all, you've really got the picture. Some people don't have much of a visible philtrum.)

Now for meanings: A very **deep** philtrum indicates that your life force energy has a strong earthy quality. Throughout your adult years, you can draw on deep reserves of sexiness. Not only does this add to your sex life. Charismatic sexual energy brings vigor to all your relationships and activities.

With **moderate** philtrum depth, you maintain a natural balance between being earthy and spiritual. Depending on circumstances, you'll draw more from one side of your nature or the other. Excellent!

With a **shallow** philtrum, you're energized mostly by your spiritual source. Not to worry, once you get turned on, you can perform as well as folks with other philtrum depths. But with this wiring of your mind-body-spirit system, you're likely to prefer quality to quantity. And your sex life won't usually matter to you as much as your spiritual life.

However you are wired for sex, respect it. Comparing yourself to others is a waste of time.

Being sexy in your way, placing sex in the context of your other strengths and interests, you can have the best possible life. Being you, just as you are right now — that is where heaven can meet earth.

48. Stress

Just how bad a fixer-upper is Cuddles anyway?

What a difference between the sexes! Women secretly plan to change men. While men secretly hope that women *won't* change. Ironically, it's women who are more apt to change; it takes a very special man to evolve voluntarily.

Stress, however, is an equal opportunity cause of change, negative change.

Stress means inner rigidity, the outcome of little problems encountered here at Earth School, such as fear, pain, and disappointment.

Coping mechanisms protect some of us from picking up stress while others stand helpless before the onslaught, filling up like vacuum cleaner bags that nobody knows how to dump. However much stress your partner has now, the amount is likely to grow, not diminish.

So do yourself a favor. Don't just make goo-goo eyes at your new boss or crush. Use your eyes (and the rest of your senses) to check out his/her level of stress.

BODY LANGUAGE

Watch **body flow** when your partner moves, gestures, and walks. Do you notice any place where his/her body seems stiff and inflexible? That corresponds to stress patterns in a specific area of life, as shown below.

Rigid neck .... Judgmental about people
Rigid hands .... Beleaguered by details
Rigid arms .... Inflexible when implementing projects
Chest stuck out ... Stress intensifies pride

Chest held in .... Stress contributes to low self-esteem
Rigid belly .... Struggling to keep life under control
Rigid shoulder .... Burdened by responsibilities
Rigid mid-back ... Inflexible follow-through on projects
Rigid low back .... Feels unsupported by others
Rigid hips .... Excessively narrow belief system
Rigid legs .... A creature of habit
Rigid knees .... Issues about dealing with authority
Rigid ankles .... Tends to tune out other people's reactions
Rigid feet .... Power has been given away to others

These are only stress patterns, remember? When released—which is always possible—you will find the opposite of the corresponding problem, e.g., A flexible neck relates to acceptance of people; flexible feet suggest living with freedom and empowerment.

Read Body Language More Fluently

When people talk about body language, they usually make it seem visual. Don't believe it.

Cues may begin visually, but that's only a trigger, a start. Your depth messages will come through your personal gift set for reading people.

For instance, looking at stress versus relaxation, perception *begins* with seeing. But that may set in motion a *physical* knowing, such as feeling your partner's tension or flexibility.

If you stop to analyze, you'll find that you have switched from seeing to feeling. You're picking up subtle shifts to muscle tone, or maybe you're sensing how the person's internal rhythm changes.

Kinesthetic perception, or knowing through your body, is a powerful gift for insight.

Do you have to *analyze* how any intuitive gift works in order to use it well? No, but you do need to trust the insights it brings.

Alternatively, looking might plunge you into the *emotions* involved. Because of the way you are wired for deeper perception, you might read emotion from the tiniest physical stiffness.

Visually, that movement could be so slight that it doesn't register consciously at all. Still, it counts. And it counts as body language.

When will you know that you're a real expert at nonverbal communication? Rules won't rule. And neither will only one sense.

You won't favor what you learn visually compared to using all your senses. (Depending on vision alone is a common mistake for beginners.) Instead, you'll read body language for whatever category you seek to investigate. Then you'll trust whatever you get.

Never do you have to analyze, "Was that a kind of inner hearing?" or "Somehow my sense of smell was involved. Is that okay?"

All your deepest knowing is connected through **synesthesia.** Your senses are wired to each other. Deeper perception comes *through* your senses, even if it seems to happen *with* your senses. That's because our knowing here at Earth School comes via human bodies. Truth comes through many holograms: body language, facial structure, patterns in aura databanks.

With synesthesia, your deep hearing connects to your deepest taste and smell and vision and knowing and feeling. So relax and enjoy it. Why use your intellect to tear apart your subtle experience?

Hey, if you had that habit drilled into you at school, turn off that ugly sounding drill.

Is your intention to access useful information? Do you, perhaps, want to help other people? Or is your main goal to give yourself a hard time?

If you're not reading body language fluently yet, you can start now: Set an intention. Read one thing at a time. Trust what you get.

And does that sound a lot like what I've taught you about aura reading? It should. Reading body language intuitively is excellent preparation for the deeper perceptions of face reading and aura reading. Trust all your senses. Trust *most* what comes most easily.

FACE READING

Sometimes you'll look at a face and think, "Here's someone who has been through a lot."

What are you seeing, exactly? Some face data commonly associated with stress really isn't.

For example, consider **down-angled eyebrows** (seen in our guy on Page 29). They really mean an intellectual gift for valuing the past.

A **down-angled mouth** (shown on Page 210, bottom) is a sign of past emotional pain that could have been healed years ago.

For more accurate indictors of long-term stress, examine four other categories.

First, notice the degree of **lower eyelid curve.** That's the bottom half of each eye, complete with the tiny eyelashes. (See Page 162.)

On most eyes, this shape curves to some degree, due to muscles that usually operate unconsciously. What causes a lower eyelid to have the default position of straight? Yep, it's stress.

Second, look for **puffs** over eyes, wads of extra flesh hanging down from the brow bone that can cover all or part of the eyelid. Puffs correspond to annoyance over little things. (You'll find one over the right eye in the illustration on Page 114, bottom right.)

On the positive side, the irascible one got that way by self-neglect, and probably has been working extra hard, either to serve others or to earn money.

Third, check for **nose grooves,** wrinkles that develop at the flanges of the nose. A nose groove is a vertical line that cuts off the nostril area.

These lines relate to resentment over lack of financial support. If the groove is on the right side, the cause was career-related, while a groove on the left suggests poverty or stinginess from family. Inner trauma leaves it mark. Before you studied physiognomy, did you think it could land on a nose?

Even after your partner heals the resentment from financial betrayal, he/she will benefit from having learned deep lessons about self-reliance.

Fourth, money worries can show in the development of **triangular nostrils.** Investigate nostril shape by looking—as always, with face reading—on the level. Do you see a pinched shape at the top of a nostril, like the apex of a triangle? (One example can be found on Page 173, bottom right illustration, left nostril only.)

That means your partner has been stressed out by financial pressure. Even when the money problems have been overcome, that nostril shape is likely to remain. Consider it major education about the value of money. That's a highly valuable kind of knowledge, even if the lesson had to be learned the hard way.

AURAS

Personal power can be severely compromised by stress. To investigate stress caused by **relationship frustration,** start with your usual Preparation Process. (See Page 25.) Set an intention to have a relaxing, enjoyable exploration.

Plug-in at the Invincibility databank at the Power Chakra and ask, "What is the balance between strength and stress?" To follow up, ask, "How does he/she respond to frustration in relationships?"

To learn about **emotional stress,** plug-in at the Emotional Balance databank at the Emotional Chakra. Ask, "What is the balance between joy and stress?"

The answers may surprise you. If you find clarity, great. If not, let your compassion grow. Where do you and your partner live anyway? It's called Earth School.

49. Stubbornness

When push comes to shove, just how stubborn is that partner of yours? Read that, if you can, *before* stubbornnesss becomes an issue at work or threatens your friendship.

BODY LANGUAGE

Walks reveal a lot about stubbornness. How does your partner *make contact* with the ground? Even wobbling along in stilettos, a walk can be more or less forceful in making contact with terra firma.

A more flatfooted walk means more stubbornness than a graceful stride.

Purposefulness is stubborn behavior in action. You can read a sample in **directness of stride.** Does your partner meander or go straight from Point A to Point B?

Balance also can show stubbornness. Is your partner, literally, a pushover? Stubborn people are not. Objectively, as well as subjectively, they hold their ground.

Next, let's turn to what I call **"situational stubbornness."** In certain situations, people change their usual amount of stubbornness. Like a mother protecting her child, or Clark Kent dressed up as Superman, anyone can temporarily act like an immoveable object.

Wouldn't you like to tell when that shift happens? Body language can warn you.

For situational stubbornness, consider yourself warned if you see at least two of the following.

+ *Forehead* shows more wrinkles than usual.
+ Eyes *glower.*
+ Eyes *narrow.*
+ Brows are *temporarily lowered* or angle downward, in knitting needle position.

+ Nostrils *flare.*
+ Breath becomes *louder,* heavier.
+ If lips are *closed,* they purse, thin or twist. Mouth angle straightens or turns down.
+ If lips are *open,* the lower teeth thrust out farther than upper teeth. Or teeth bare in a snarl.
+ Jaws *tighten.*
+ The chin wrinkles or shows temporary *dimples.*
+ Head moves to angle the chin *upward.*
+ Neck moves to thrust the head *forward.*
+ The body visibly *tenses.*
+ Arms are folded to *cover* the solar plexus or heart.

So many nonverbal ways to give you the same advice: Back off!

Depending on how you handle the situation, you'll see your partner relax. Any of these warning signs can change back to normal just as quickly as it first appeared. Good luck!

FACE READING

Does stubbornness show in face data? That puts it mildly.

Let's begin with **earlobe size.** Larger lobes correlate with being stubborn. (You'll see an *average-sized* earlobe on Page 192, right side, while a *large* earlobe shows in the drawing on the left. For a *small* earlobe, you'll find a sample on Page 183, top left)

Check next to see if earlobes are **puffy.** That's different from overall size. Most lobes have the same texture as the rest of the ear, but on some folks they seems permanently swollen.

Very puffy earlobes also protrude, so while seeing a face from the front, even with in-angled ears, earlobes will stick out noticeably.

Puffiness corresponds to street smarts combined with intense stubbornness (and, possibly, bullying). This stubborn person definitely knows how to get his/her way.

Another trademark of stubbornness is **earlobe shape,** which sym-bolizes a person's subconscious way of relating to Mother Nature.

+ Most lobes are *curved,* suggesting a heart-felt love of life.

+ *Straight* earlobes convey an intellectual way of connecting to the environment, often a desire to work for abstract or altruistic principles (e.g., preserving the environment).

+ *Triangular* earlobes, however, reveal something less altruistic. What matters most about one's environment is staying in control of it. Depending on the person's agenda, that could be good or bad. What's certain, however, is resolve.

If you fuss over this person's motives or actions, what will hap-pen? The resulting show of stubbornness may take your breath away.

Yet another variety of stubbornness shows in a **diamond-shaped face** (widest at the cheeks, tapering toward forehead as well as chin), which correlates with the survivor power style. Nobody can break this person's spirit, though a few have probably tried.

Finally, **wide jaws** (pictured on Page 89) reveal stubbornness. If you become involved with a wide-jawed partner, this attribute can work to your advantage.

Annoying though it may be sometimes to deal with his/her stubborn qualities, a promise is tucked into those jaws. They go with a marvellous talent for commitment. No other item of face data means more about staying power for your relationship.

AURAS

"Why research this? I'm not stubborn," you may protest.

Everyone is, though. "Stubborn" can be a short way to say, "This person really cares deeply about a particular person/cause/aspect of life." Think of your greatest personal heroes. Are they stubborn or what?

So if you find a person's greatest area of stubbornness, you're on to something great… as well as something potentially annoying.

That annoying aspect is linked to the shadow side of stubbornness which, of course, is caused by STUFF.

Auras can help you to research both aspects of stubbornness, sunshine and shadow. Start at the Idealism databank at the Power Chakra.

Do your usual Preparation Process. (See Page 25.) Set an intention to learn the truth about this person. Ask, "What gift does he/she have for staying power when challenged."

For follow-up, explore the Patterns of Defensiveness databank at that same chakra. Ask, "How does he/she respond if contradicted?"

Depending on your particular situation, you might choose to read this same pair of databanks, and the same questions, at other chakras:

+ The Communication Chakra will reveal verbal style expressing stubbornness.
+ The Spiritual Chakra can inform you about religious stubbornness.
+ The Physical Chakra brings messages about physical staying power.
+ And the Sexual Chakra may inspire you with insights about artistic stubbornness.

Research away and you'll find plenty to admire, plus cautions about treading lightly. And speaking of which....

I hope you often have found that, after doing research suggested by this book, you have wanted to share your discoveries about the fine points of your partner's aura. But consider yourself warned:

Whatever you learn about stubbornness, keep it to yourself. Otherwise you're sure to generate more of the same. Out will come that shadow side, unless the two of you happen to be standing together on your back porch, watching pigs fly.

50. Trust

Relax and read it. Trust is one of the few attributes where, with patience, you can succeed at changing your partner.

BODY LANGUAGE

Crossing gestures reveal lack of trust. They need not go so far as having your partner make the sign of the cross and wave a wreath of garlic. A simple *leg cross* will do. Trust decreases in direct proportion to the height of the gesture.

Thus, *crossed ankles* indicate polite reserve.

One *foot over a knee* signifies deeper skepticism—the below-belt equivalent of a raised eyebrow.

A *leg crossed at the knee* bespeaks greater wariness (unless the leg-crosser is showing off great gams).

The prize for pent-up trust goes to *The Knot*, when arms are crossed, then placed over a knee that, itself, has been placed atop a pair of crossed legs. The Knot means that he/she does KNOT trust you. (For more about crossing gestures, see Page 203.)

On faces, relaxation corresponds to trust, while **facial tension** suggests the opposite. Check out the jaws, mouth, eyes, and eyebrows.

Although these body language clues are dependable, don't stop your trust research there.

FACE READING

In sticky situations, whom does your partner trust enough to ask for help? Read the answer in two contrasting **wrinkles around eyes**.

Does he/she turn to others? Over time, this results in lines that stretch **outward** at the eyes' outer corners. Commonly called "crow's feet," these eye extenders show trust, especially during trying times. He/she will reach out for support and ideas.

By contrast, circles and bags **under** eyes symbolize looking within. Big ones belong to introspective folks, life's philosophers and poets.

So it's significant which type of eye wrinkle dominates. If they're equal, your partner places trust equally in both directions.

What does it mean when somebody aged 30+ lacks any eye wrinkles? Whether through cosmetic surgery or skin that's naturally permanent press, he/she leads a relatively carefree life.

This could be due to spiritual grandeur or shallowness. I'd make it my business to find out, wouldn't you? Of course, that means reading auras.

AURAS

For the most dependable way to fathom your partner's depth of living, or depth of trust, read auras. Begin with your usual Preparation Process: Pay attention to your inner awareness, then Get Big and set an intention to gain more wisdom. (For more details, see Page 25.)

Plug-in at the Confidence databank in the Power Chakra. Ask, "Does he/she feel more or less powerful when trusting other people?"

Follow up by asking, "Does he/she feel more or less powerful when trusting *me?*"

Trust may be a big issue for your partner. If you suspect a problem, plug-in at other Confidence databanks. (They're in all the main chakras pictured inside the cover.) Repeat the same two questions.

Sometimes you'll find trust issues in just one aspect of life. Consider yourself forewarned to go easy. For instance, if there's a problem with trust at the Communication Chakra, don't push your partner to talk to you.

And when he/she finally does speak up, even if it's the first time in months, even if you're so excited that you can hardly keep from jumping up and down, screaming "Whoopee!" — just stop and take a deep breath. If you'd like your partner's trust to grow, express your interest *gently*.

And what about you? As you gain experience and clear STUFF from your aura, you'll increasingly trust your deeper perception which, in turn, can help you to trust life more.

Now you have the tools to distinguish a great business proposition from a get-rich-quick scheme, separate true love from a fantasy, and more.

But what takes the greatest trust of all? Falling in love takes enormous trust. Yet staying with a partner, deepening your love over time, surely that demands a greater trust. Dare to build a life with the one who's right for you.

10 Rules for a Love Relationship

Now that you've read your partner (and yourself), do you feel great about your closest personal relationship? What if you have loads of compatibilities, share basic values, and love each passionately... but you're still not getting along? The problem could involve 10 very basic social skills. How do you rate at using them?

1. DON'T GOSSIP

Is your love relationship important to you? Then don't dilute it by talking behind his/her back, complaining or telling secrets that are part of **your special life together.**

2. DO STAND UNITED

Present a **united front,** not only in front of any children but before relatives, friends, and anyone else you meet in public.

If you're going to argue, do it privately. By letting others see you as a happy couple, they'll expect good things of your relationship, which can become a powerful self-fulfilling prophesy.

3. DON'T CRITICIZE

Your habits of treating others become your habits of treating your-self. Besides, kvetching means one of the following:

+ You have **unfinished business.** This is not something to blame on your partner.
+ You grew up in an atmosphere of **criticism.** (How much sense does it make to pass along *that* family heirloom?)
+ You've forgotten to be **grateful** for your blessings. If you can't get over the habit of criticism, find someone to help.
+ You and your partner need to work on your **communication** style. Criticism stands all the way at the bottom of the list of ways to communicate well. It is an ineffective — frankly, a doomed—way to change anything.

4. DO PRAISE

Use **sincere praise** to reinforce behavior that you like. Actively look for things to praise, giving your partner sincere compliments when possible.

What if anger seeps through your well chosen words, turning smiles into snarls? Pleasant behavior with rage beneath won't fool anyone. So get help, if needed, to clear out the backlog.

5. DON'T MAKE HIM/HER YOUR WHOLE LIFE

Your partner doesn't need that kind of pressure. Neither do you. Make your main relationship stronger by **cultivating other friendships** and interests. Interact with real people, not just the thin slice on the Net. Connect to spiritual source regularly. Being balanced, you'll have a better love life.

6. DO SPEND QUALITY TIME TOGETHER

You can't keep a relationship lively by remote control. There is no equivalent of a TV clicker for turning on love. Speaking of TV, please spend some time each day without the mind-numbing thing flickering in the background. Eat at least one meal together, if possible. And **connect** daily by having a conversation where both of you give each other undivided attention.

7. DON'T SETTLE

Behavior that hurts you, like physical or verbal abuse, is not acceptable. "But I love him/her." is no reason to stay in a relationship where you're being hurt.

If your own body language shows that you feel like a victim, change it. **Walk tall**, which happens to be your birthright.

8. DO ACCEPT

So maybe your lover isn't **100% perfect** yet. Maybe you're not, either. By showing appreciation for what you've got, you'll make it better.

Nurturing the good will bring better results than complaining about the bad. With all the ways this book gives you to read your lover, you can find ample evidence that your mate is different from you. Vive la différence!

9. DON'T COERCE

What is the most widespread destructive psychic force on the planet? **Psychic coercion.** People send it out whenever they repeatedly think, pray, or talk about how they want someone else to change.

When do you have the right to intervene in someone else's life? Illegal behavior shouldn't be tolerated; children under 18 should be guided. Otherwise, you have no right to outline how anyone else's life should show up.

What if, for example, you hate your partner's taste in socks? Say so once, then let it go. No need to coerce, or turn sockastic.

10. DO ASK FOR WHAT YOU NEED AND WANT

Did you hook up with your partner because he/she was a mind reader? Probably not, so why assume that he/she always knows what would make you happy?

It doesn't take nearly so much work for *you* to figure out what you want and need, then express it.

What is the difference between a want and a need, anyway?

The former is nice but optional while the latter is imperative.

+ For example, how many times a week do you **need** to make love?
+ What kinds of touch fall into the **want** category—fun but not required for you to feel satisfied?
+ What is one thing you **want** to do with money, just for fun?
+ And what do you **need** to do with money, so that you feel secure?
+ Is being listened to by your lover something you just **want** once in a while, or is it something you **need** to have on a regular basis?

Forget "normal." Be honest with yourself.

I know, that can be hard. And asking can be even harder. When asking, you may feel vulnerable. Still, a love relationship should be the safest place in the world for both of you to express what you need and want.

So ask politely, expecting a positive response.

Also do what is humanly possible to fulfill requests from your partner to you, making his/her needs a high priority.

Now that you can read deeper, do you see the potential? From the most intimate desires of your soul all the way up to the surface, **you and your partner can make life glorious.**

Relationship Reading List

BOOKS

Armstrong, Thomas, Ph.D., *7 Kinds of Smart: Identifying and Developing Your Multiple Intelligences, Revised and Updated with Information on 2 New Kinds of Smart* (New York: Plume, 1993).

Aron, Elaine, Ph.D., *The Highly Sensitive Person: How to Thrive When the World Overwhelms You* (Seacaucus, N.J.: Birch Lane Press, 1996).

Bates, Brian et al., *The Human Face* (New York: Dorling Kindersley, 2001).

Dimitrius, Joe-Ellan, *Reading People: How to Understand People and Predict Their Behavior, Anytime, Anyplace* (NY: Ballantine, 1999).

Fast, J., *The Body Language of Sex, Power and Aggression* (NY: M. Evans, 1977).

Gladwell, M., *The Tipping Point* (Boston: Little, Brown, 2000).

Goffman, E., *The Presentation of Self in Everyday Life* (NY: Anchor Books, 1969).

Lloyd-Elliott, Martin, *Secrets of Sexual Body Language* (Berkeley, CA: Ulysses Press, 1994).

Tennov, D. Love and Limerance, *The Experience of Being in Love* (NY: Stein and Day, 1980).

Hay, L., *Heal Your Body: The Mental Causes for Physical Illness and the Metaphysical Way to Overcome Them* (Santa Monica, CA: Hay House, 1988).

ARTICLES

John Gottman et al., "Facial Expressions During Marital Conflict," Journal of Family Communication (2000), vol.1, no. 1, pp. 37 – 57.

H. Friedman et al., "Understanding and Assessing Nonverbal Expressiveness: The Affective Communication Test," *Journal of Personality and Social Psychology* (1980), vol. 39, no. 2, pp. 333-351.

H. Friedman and R. Riggio, "Effect of Individual Differences in Nonverbal Expressiveness on Transmission of Emotion," *Journal of Nonverbal Behavior* (Winter 1981), vol. 6, pp. 96-104.

G. Wells and R. Petty, "The Effects of Overt Head Movements on Persuasion," *Basic and Applied Social Psychology* (1980), vol. 1, no. 3, pp. 219-230.

BOOKS BY ROSE ROSETREE

Available through Women's Intuition Worldwide, LLC

Cut Cords of Attachment: Heal Yourself and Others with Energy Spirituality
This is a how-to and also a consumer guide for healing imbalances in your emotional and spiritual life. Presenting leading-edge techniques, this book can help you to read those 50 databanks in any chakra. Rose's book was the first in English on the topic of cutting cords, summarizing 20 years of experience as a healing practitioner.

Aura Reading Through All Your Senses
Here Rose pioneers her easy-to-learn method of Aura Reading Through All Your Senses®. This book shows how aura reading can improve relationships, health, even your choices as a consumer. The how-to includes over 100 techniques.

Empowered by Empathy
Rosetree's book was the first to show how to use spiritual awareness to turn inborn gifts OFF or ON at will. This contrasts with more common approaches, behavior based, such as "strengthen your boundaries." Energy Spirituality uses the power of consciousness to bring empaths cumulative empowerment and true peace of mind. (Both Print and Audiobook Editions are available.)

Let Today Be a Holiday: 365 Ways to Co-Create with God
Add to your skill set with over 450 techniques, plus thought-provoking ideas. *Holiday* is a daybook. But you can also browse at will, strengthening your connection to your most important relationship of all, the one with your spiritual Source.

The Roar of the Huntids (A Novel for Empaths)
This spiritual thriller is a coming-of-age story about Energy Spirituality. Set in the year 2020, the story is spiced with social and political satire, plus a fast-moving plot, romance, and quirky characters (some of whom are empaths and some who are definitely not).

The Power of Face Reading
Rosetree has been called "The mother of American physiognomy." Her system of Face Reading Secrets® presents soulful interpretations of physical face data, with nuanced but highly accurate readings about personal style — an easy, useful reference book with over 100 illustrations. It's like a birdwatcher's guide for people.

Wrinkles Are God's Makeup: How You Can Find Meaning in Your Evolving Face
In the 5,000-year history of reading faces for character, this is the first to explore how faces change over time. Using comparison photos, you learn to become a spiritual talent scout.

Order books at the author's website, www.rose-rosetree.com.

Bookstores and libraries: WIW distributors include New Leaf, Baker & Taylor, Ingram, Quality Books.

Many of Rose Rosetree's titles are available in foreign editions. For purchasing information contact Women's Intuition Worldwide, LLC.

If you are a publisher or distributor outside the U.S., interested in foreign rights acquisitions, contact our literary agent, Deanna Leah, President of HBG Productions, deanna@hbgproductions.com, available by telephone at 530-893-4699.

INDEX 1. BODY LANGUAGE

INDEX 2. FACE READING

INDEX 3. AURAS

Rose Rosetree says, *"Go ahead, read me. You know how."*

Her how-to books (including a
national bestseller in Germany)
and blog, "Deeper Perception
Made Practical," are available
at www.rose-rosetree.com.

Over the past 38 years,
this Brandeis graduate
has given more than
800 media interviews.

Clients include Long
& Foster, Canyon
Ranch, The Food
Marketing Insti-
tute, George
Washington
University, The
Inner Potential
Centre, USA
Today, and
VOICE.